RED, GREEN, AND SOMETIMES BEIGE

RED, GREEN, AND SOMETIMES BEIGE

The Ins and Outs of a Healthy Relationship

Kasturi Mahanta

SIMON &
SCHUSTER

London · New York · Sydney · Toronto · New Delhi

First published in India by Simon & Schuster India, 2024

1 3 5 7 9 10 8 6 4 2

Simon & Schuster India
818, Indraprakash Building,
21, Barakhamba Road,
New Delhi 110001

www.simonandschuster.co.in

Paperback ISBN: 978-81-978920-3-5

eBook ISBN: 978-81-978920-8-0

Simon & Schuster: Celebrating 100 Years of Publishing in 2024

Typeset in India by SŪRYA, New Delhi
Printed and bound in India by Replika Press Pvt. Ltd.

To Lily, who introduced me to the power of books and unknowingly also taught me the beauty of a safe relationship.

Thank you, Aita. :)

Contents

Author's Note

Hi there! I wanted to let you know that while this book draws from my years of working with many wonderful individuals, all the characters and situations are fictionalised. These aren't my clients' stories—confidentiality is super important to me. Any similarities to real people or events are completely coincidental. Also understand that while this book can be used as a self-discovery tool, it is not a substitute for real-time therapy, nor can it be considered a substitute for individualised medical diagnosis or treatment.

Introduction

Pyaar, ishq, aur mohabbat…jo bhi inka naam le, pehle dil ko thaam le.

Love, romance, and affection—anybody who says these words will first have to clutch their hearts.

This was my idea of relationships growing up. And of course, Shah Rukh Khan coming back to Kajol after days of being MIA and romancing in yellow fields was a visual that became the epitome of what a relationship looks like. Naturally, the visual became an emblem of romance for me too. I tried to emulate this ideal in my first few serious relationships, only to find them all ending in failure. I ended up either with a broken heart or being cast as the villain. This was not the love I had imagined. It certainly wasn't what they showed in the movies. What the hell was I doing wrong?

This question saved my life, even though I asked it quite late. But as they say, der aaye durust aaye (better late than never), right?

Don't get me wrong. I am a hardcore romantic. I believe in all the wonders romance has to offer—the roses, the coffee dates, the fairy lights, and the waves crashing in the background. I am even up for a bit of salsa in a yellow saree in Switzerland. That is romance, yes, and it's needed. But as an Indian girl growing up in Assam in the 90s, schooled in an all-girls institution, with an elder brother acting as my third parent, I was most interested in topics I was forced to stay away from: love and boys.

These topics were taboo. There was no concept of dating. Even mentioning boys and relationships or love was unthinkable. As a curious teenager, the only sources of information for me in the early 2000s were the TV and radio, and a lot of things (very crucial things) were left up to the imagination. Anything remotely intimate in the movies used to be censored by either the Censor Board or by my parents. The agony aunt sections in magazines like *Women's Era*, *Reader's Digest*, and *The Telegraph* were the only places where we could get more information about love and relationships.

The lack of open dialogue and insufficient portrayal of what open conversations, love, and relationships *actually* entail led me to develop half-baked ideas of what an ideal romance looked like or what marriage is supposed to mean. And I thought I knew it all. I thought I was completely prepared.

But didn't poet Jigar Moradabadi put it aptly? Ye ishq nahi asaan bas itna samajh lijiye / Ek aag ka dariya hai aur doob ke jaana hai (Understand that this love is not easy / It's a river of fire and one must drown in it).

Well, it looks like he was in need of a relationship expert to break things down for him too.

Young me saw myself in the throes of a beautiful relationship that brought with it the beauty of love and romance—the chocolates, the impromptu dates, the rainy drives—but along with it came intense fights, name-calling, teary nights, and confusion. Confusion about why relationships weren't as beautiful as I imagined. Was I not the right person for a relationship? Was this the right person for me? Did this relationship even make me feel good? Why were there so many fights, so many tears, and so much heartache?

As I moved on with my limited knowledge and fixed beliefs about love and romance, life saw me in and out of several relationships. Several *failed* relationships. Then one day, I stopped. I had to make sense of it all. I had to understand why I was failing in relationships while thriving in all other areas of my life. Was my knight in shining armour a myth? Was I expecting too much from the wrong person? Was I the toxic one? Were they narcissists? How could I fall for people who treated me that way? How could I let this happen to me?

I reached a point where I transitioned from having a dreamy, romantic definition of relationships to equating them with something to steer clear of. I couldn't imagine getting my heart broken again after it had already been shattered multiple times. From a braveheart ready to burn in the flames of love, I had become a weary traveller who just wanted to be left alone.

Heartbreak had won, and I had lost.

But it was that one particularly bad heartbreak, which had left me so worn out, that forced me to question it all. My choices in partners. The way I showed up in these relationships. What was my idea of being in a relationship? What did commitment really mean? What was growth in a relationship? Was it possible to grow in a relationship at all? For the first time in a long, long time, I started being conscious of what love can actually do and what relationships might actually mean.

This is where my journey began. I immersed myself in *understanding* relationships. I recognised that avoiding a lot of my blunders indeed was possible. What I was experiencing was just a series of one uninformed decision after another. There was a reason behind my choices, behind the way I craved love and never seemed to receive it, why I couldn't communicate my needs or wants, and why I always felt unfulfilled in romantic relationships. I also realised that no one could teach me all of this growing up. There were no technical terminologies or scientific explanations associated with relationships. It was just considered something that happened.

But no, healthy relationships are built on a series of conscious decisions. You cannot just wing relationships.

I went back to studying and got my Masters in Psychology followed by a specialisation in Marriage and Family Therapy. I studied hard and studied deeply. I was passionately seeking answers to the hundreds of questions in my head.

Slowly but steadily, I started to understand how our choices in present romantic relationships have so much to do with our childhood experiences, how there exist different attachment styles and how we might be speaking French while our partner understands Hindi.

My journey into understanding relationships has been long and tumultuous. But it need not be the same for you. A basic understanding of relationships and their complexities is something I want you to be equipped with.

In fact, the relationship pillar is a very important pillar which influences other areas of our life as well. No man is an island, and our needs in relationships ought to be understood by us so that we can make better choices and build healthier, conscious relationships.

As I began counselling people, I realised that clients were coming to me too late. It was either when they were already applying for divorce or, in the case of individuals, when they had already broken up or been in toxic, abusive relationships for way too long. This is when I discerned that even now, education when it comes to love and relationships, is completely missing. Where do people learn from? How do they understand the difference between toxic, unhealthy, and healthy relationships? Even though we had progressed from my age of TV and radio to the age of the Internet, people were now getting crucial information from places like Reddit, Quora, and Cosmo.

I decided to spread knowledge about this so that people could understand and build healthy relationships before feeling completely defeated by them. This is how my Instagram page, *@heymisstherapist*, started.

I began discussing relationships, communication techniques, attachment styles, and more, and people responded. The gap in formal education around relationships was glaringly obvious.

Over the past few years, I have built a community of people who genuinely want to be more conscious of their communication, needs and wants, and show up as their most authentic selves in life and relationships. This is something I would have benefited from growing up, and I am glad I can bridge this gap.

Every day, I counsel individuals and couples from all over the world—some trying to make their relationships work, others seeking to have difficult conversations and learn how to show up better. Young adults come to me when they are just starting their dating journey, and some come to me when they are ready to take the next step in the relationship but want to learn how to iron out the kinks. Then there are others who are trying to find their footing in love and their identities. I am glad to say that there is something for everyone in this book. I love being able to help people by teaching them tools and techniques to deal with these problems on their own and sharing perspectives and methodologies so that they can tackle the hurdles with resilience and hope, empowering them to take decisions that align with their long-term vision.

I hope you enjoy reading this book. I believe it is essential for everyone's library, offering much-needed technical knowledge about relationships. Often, we are expected to nurture and maintain healthy relationships, much like a gardener helps flowers bloom, but we lack the proper tools to succeed. This book aims to fill that gap.

I have made a concerted effort to keep the content relatable and straightforward while ensuring that important terminologies are clearly explained. My goal is to equip you with the language and understanding needed to articulate your thoughts, needs, and perspectives effectively in any relationship. Whether you are communicating with yourself, your partner, or your therapist, this book will provide you with the tools to do so.

Relationships are complex, and having the right knowledge can make all the difference. This book offers insights and practical advice that will empower you to navigate the intricacies of your relationships with confidence. By the end of this book, you will feel better prepared to cultivate and sustain healthy, fulfilling relationships.

Thank you for allowing this book to be a part of your journey.

Chapter 1

Chemistry vs Compatibility

The Great Debate

'I am going to break up with him today,' she thinks, putting on the reddest lipstick she can find in her vanity.

'But what if he changes?' a small voice whispers in her right ear. Her lips look bold, but her inner resolve doesn't match it.

'It has been fucking 14 months, he hasn't changed till now, has he, Misha?' a harsher voice whispers in her left ear. Her phone rang, drowning the voices.

'Ready for the big day?' Anusha starts. Anusha has known her for 10 years now and has witnessed the ups and downs of most of her dating life.

'Yes, yes!!!' Misha exclaims, faking her confusion. 'As ready as I can be. It's going to be a bad day for Rohit.'

'Chal, come over to my place when you are done. Shall I ask Didi to make something specific?'

Misha refuses. 'Let's order when I get there? Okay, bye.'

'All the best!' Anusha quips, before hanging up.

Misha looks at the phone screen. Her wallpaper is of a trip to Bali she took with Rohit just a few months ago.

It was a great one. All their trips are great. He is the most caring, protective, and thoughtful person on these trips. And the sex? Oof, the sex is great!

But when they are back? He goes completely MIA for days, there is always something up at work or in the family that requires his complete attention. But somehow, he always has time for his friends—hanging out at clubs and making appearances at late-night parties. She only comes to know through Instagram, of course. But after she confronts him about it, she can't even see the updates anymore. Maybe she has been blocked? Maybe he is truly busy?

Rohit says he wants to get married, but that's only when he is *really* drunk. Misha loves that part of him—he becomes so open, vulnerable, and emotional. That is the Rohit she is truly in love with. But apart from those rare occasions, he is quiet, emotionally withdrawn, and rarely talks of the future or commitment, let alone marriage. Rohit is busy, and she gets it; she is busy as well. A demanding job and an ambitious career have taken up most of their time, but she does remember Rohit every day, every moment actually. But Rohit thinks of it otherwise. He doesn't really call much, and texts only intermittently. He says he needs his space and is very consumed with work at all times. Misha understands and tries to give him the space he needs. She is not the clingy, always-on-the-phone, always-texting kind of girlfriend. Or is she?

She isn't sure of anything anymore. And that bothers her so much. Her life can't be just sex-filled weekend trips to beautiful islands filled with sand and booze. Yes, that sounds great and feels even better, but she is 32, looking for marriage, and wants cute children. Or at least a dog? Rohit seemed to be on the same page at first. Fourteen

Would you believe if I say that a lot of us get into relationships that already have the potential to turn unhealthy?

I need you to understand something important if you want to avoid this—the concept of needs. When you know you are not getting what you want, but you stay in a connection for the potential it has and hope that it will change one day—without having valid proof or facts—it is a sure-shot recipe for a lot of hurt and disappointment.

One of the biggest problems is that a lot of us are not clear about our needs in a romantic relationship. We do not prioritise our practical needs of connection, intimacy, monogamy, and trust amongst others, and tend to harp on 'chemistry'.

Needs have been in the picture forever but was popularised by Maslow (Maslow, A. H. (1943). A Theory of Human Motivation. *Psychological Review, 50*(4), 370–396) when he decided to categorise our needs into five basic criteria, namely physiological needs, need for safety, love and belonging, esteem, and self-actualisation.

And accurately so.

From a relationship POV, needs in a relationship can look like:

1. Feeling supported
2. Having a safe space to be vulnerable and feel secure
3. Accountability
4. Consistency
5. Honesty
6. Intimacy
7. Growth

8. Validation
9. Support
10. Feeling loved, accepted, and wanted for our true essence and who we truly are.

Everybody's needs do not look the same. Nor do they hold the same priority. You may prioritise physical intimacy over financial support and that is completely okay. But for someone else, a growth mindset and validation might be a priority instead.

Needs are neither right nor wrong. They are what they are—needs. When our needs are fulfilled, we feel happy, satisfied, content, and hopeful. When our needs are minimised, dismissed, trivialised, invalidated, or unmet, we might feel bitter, sad, resentful, and confused.

Misha is confused and is in a cycle of suffering because she is not sure of her needs. Weirdly enough, the cycle of invalidating our needs might start with us. In most cases, we are the first ones to minimise and dismiss our own needs. We might feel we are not worthy enough of getting our needs met and somewhere deep down believe that either they can't be met or that our needs are just not as important as somebody else's needs.

Misha consciously wants commitment, consistency, and a future together with Rohit more than anything else—that means a few of her core needs would roughly translate to wanting a serious relationship, marriage or further commitment, vocalised affection, and physical intimacy. But when Rohit and she get together, she becomes overwhelmed by the present—great electrifying physical chemistry and words that feel like music to her ears—and she wanders far away from her core needs. In the process, she may possibly be sending mixed signals too, allowing Rohit to believe that her needs actually are being met, or she is getting what she is looking for. This is a sure-shot recipe for an unhealthy romance.

Identifying needs is important because it can decide what your life looks like—not just a relationship but also your career, family, finances, friendships, and other bonds.

A great indicator of not being sure of our needs is when we let another person take the driver's seat and get behind the wheel of our life. We lament about not reaching where we want to go, all the while not assessing whether the person behind the driver's wheel is adept or qualified enough to get us to our goal, or even has the willingness to take us there. Instead, we are clueless about why they are taking detours and unnecessarily long routes, and while we are confused, we also start enjoying the unexpected turns. The newness feels good and keeps us wishing for more. We also fear that if we complain we might be thrown out of the car altogether. We'd much rather be on a road trip, *any* roadtrip, than to have no fun at all. And that is where the never-ending loop of confusion and excitement starts. We don't understand why we are dissatisfied after a while.

Sometimes we end up invalidating our own needs because we do not have enough clarity and end up getting carried away by whatever is in front of us. Imagine you want to get on a flight that helps you reach Italy in five hours and is a direct flight. But when you log on to a website to book your tickets, you see that there are 10 other options that are visibly cheaper, with better airlines, or are at a much more convenient time.

What do you choose?

- *Option 1*—A compromise on the total journey time and on the airline experience = low prices
- *Option 2*—convenient time + less travel time + a great experience = a hole in your pocket

If you are not very sure of your actual need in the first place, you will probably end up choosing Option 1 because it helps you save some money, and it sounds lucrative in the moment. You see yourself spending all of the saved money on extra paninis and gelatos once you are in Italy. But that is only true in your head.

Choosing to invalidate your need for a direct flight has other implications. You end up experiencing an unnecessarily long journey full of multiple security checks and layovers, even though you had the finances to invest in a direct flight in the first place.

It is very similar to the romantic experiences in our life. We meet someone, we do not have much clarity nor confidence over what is it that we exactly need or our criteria for selection. We are overwhelmed by whatever is presented in front of us and tend to wing it, crossing our fingers and hoping that it is the right choice for us. But what happens next?

Our narratives don't match, we speak different languages, and can't seem to understand each other or see eye to eye on values and beliefs. Once the initial flutters wear off, it becomes more and more evident to us that we might be expecting different things. Then, we can either choose to let the relationship remain the same—filled with unspoken expectations and growing resentment—or leave, hoping to have a better relationship the next time, only to make similar choices again. Or we can choose to work on identifying our needs and vocalising them, making sure of what it is that we want and how acknowledging those would be beneficial for the relationship.

EXERCISE 1: IDENTIFY YOUR NEEDS

I hate it when...and instead

Visualise what irks you or puts you off the most in a relationship. You can take into consideration your previous relationships, any relationship you have closely witnessed, or go deeper within. Go ahead and write at least 10 situations that start with **'I hate it when…'**or **'I would hate it if my partner…'** Once you have those 10 sentences written out, continue to expand on them by adding these words: 'Instead if they would…' and allow yourself to complete the sentence.

Example: I hate it when they talk over me. Instead, they could just be patient and listen to me, without interruption.

Here your needs can translate to valuing patience, empathy, and compassion.

Be as honest as you possibly can be, without any judgment or preconceived notions.

EXERCISE 2: PRIORITISE YOUR NEEDS

From the list below, choose a maximum of **10 needs** that you think are your **top priority.** I know you might be tempted to choose all, but remember to prioritise. Otherwise, it just adds to numerous options.

- Love
- Trust
- Communication
- Intimacy
- Support
- Connection
- Respect
- Understanding
- Affection
- Security
- Autonomy
- Empathy
- Appreciation
- Validation
- Time
- Shared Values
- Belonging
- Comfort
- Encouragement
- Fulfillment
- Openness
- Companionship
- Patience
- Honesty
- Loyalty
- Emotional Safety
- Partnership
- Playfulness
- Quality Time
- Independence
- Shared Goals

- Physical Touch
- Affirmation
- Acceptance
- Nurturing

Once you have your needs sorted, it is time to understand another common roadblock that leads to unhealthy relationships—commonly seen as the secret sauce and holy grail of romance—chemistry.

Chemistry is very closely associated with a romantic relationship. In fact, at times we might even use it interchangeably with compatibility or love. But what is chemistry, really?

Is chemistry the banter George Clooney exchanged with Julia Roberts on the sidewalk in *Pretty Woman*? Or when Shah Rukh Khan and Kajol both sat outside, locked out of the train compartment in *Dilwale Dulhaniya Le Jayenge*? Or is it defined by the sultriness of Bipasha Basu and John Abraham in *Jism*? Can *Silsila* be called the epitome of chemistry—chemistry so strong that even after marriage destiny brings two lovers together?

Chemistry is all of this, yes. But chemistry is also so much more than just this. Unfortunately, most of us are just hung up on pop-culture narratives to define chemistry for us in our real-life romances. We glorify every gesture that gives us the faintest hints of romance and downplay or take for granted anything that doesn't fit the story we are weaving.

Chemistry is aptly named because it IS 'chemistry'. So to understand chemistry in romantic relationships, let me give you a tiny chemistry lesson on brain chemicals that are responsible for the chemistry you feel in your heart and other places—and yes, pay attention because this chemistry class is actually of use.

Chemistry is really a mixture of hormones (testosterone and estrogen) and neurotransmitters (dopamine and serotonin). Dopamine, serotonin, and norepinephrine help determine if you are initially attracted to someone.

- **Dopamine** is released when you are love-struck (the stage where we feel captivated by feelings of love and find it hard to focus on anything else), and positive reinforcement causes more dopamine to flow—a rush of happiness from feeling rewarded and reciprocated follow. Dopamine activates the reward circuit, helping to make love a pleasurable experience, similar to the euphoria associated with use of cocaine or alcohol.
- As dopamine levels rise, so does **serotonin**—our happy hormones are now in full swing—and we might feel like running around, humming the tunes to our favourite love song or giggle and laugh and feel happier and more positive than we usually would. Add **norepinephrine**—the chemical that helps your body respond to stress by increasing heart rate and alertness ensures that we have clouds under our feet and sleepless nights in love.
- **Oxytocin** helps form bonds and attachments and also reshapes your brain when you are in love. Oxytocin is called the 'cuddle chemical', because it is released, for example, when a mother cuddles her baby or when we are affectionate and

cuddling or having sex with somebody we're in a romantic partnership with, or even somebody that we're having sex with but are not in a romantic partnership with.

- Apart from these, our sex hormones, **testosterone** and **estrogen**, drive lust and sexual attraction, and mixed with everything else, forms a heady concoction of romance, attachment, intimacy, and lust. A concoction that is extremely addictive and we can't seem to get enough of it.

Chemistry reflects in the way you laugh with your partner, or smile remembering them, how you both express the exact same emotions for that 80s track, or how both of your bodies speak in bed.

But does better chemistry mean that there are higher chances that a relationship will be fulfilling? Absolutely not. **High chemistry ≠ High compatibility.**

Misha has seemingly great chemistry with Rohit. But then why does she want to break up with him? It is because, in reality, there are many more things required to actually foster a healthy relationship than just great chemistry.

Compatibility is the alignment of lifestyle choices and values of two people. Compatibility can reflect in the form of life goals, values, and belief systems. It is when both partners believe art is essential for mankind and agree on the same kind of music, or their idea of a great vacation is the trip from the kitchen to the bed on weekends.

One of the most important pillars of compatibility is values. Having the same definition of honesty, authenticity, ethics, safety, and security is a big and important chunk of compatibility in a romantic relationship. Being on the same page about (most) things that matter to an individual for living a happy and secure life is compatibility.

Low Compatibility/Low Chemistry These connections do not usually go anywhere. People on dating apps where a conversation doesn't move beyond two days, or dates which feel '"bleh' fall into this category.	**Low Compatibility/High Chemistry** This is where disaster occurs. The chemistry is amazing and there is no compatibility—meaning intensity of emotions exists without being on the same page about a lot of things. This is where most unhealthy and toxic relationships and trauma bonds exist.
High Compatibility/Low Chemistry A relationship that fulfils you in many aspects but lacks spontaneity or sexuality. This is where many platonic relationships and friendships also exist. A romantic relationship in this category might not exactly feel like *sparks flying*	**High Compatibility/High Chemistry** A divine combination. Like the tartness of berries with smooth dark chocolate. You just can't get enough, nor can you get bored. This relationship is a mix of great intimacy balanced with viability.

But the truth is, relationships are not exactly a dark chocolate mousse with berry compote. In fact, far from it. There are no exact measurements nor moulds that can help us get accurate results every time, nor can we predict the outcome. Relationships are messy and unpredictable—because they consist of complex humans—hence understanding how compatibility and chemistry work can help us at least inch closer to the results we want to achieve.

Focusing on just chemistry can result in a very unfulfilled relationship, where only bodies and emotions speak but you cannot see eye-to-eye on several everyday matters. A healthy relationship requires a safe space to be vulnerable and have intimate conversations that bare your true emotions and feelings, and also hold space for difficult conversations that lead to growth. With just crackling chemistry, safe spaces might take a backseat. Safe spaces might even feel 'boring'.

Chemistry is addictive. Dopamine and serotonin makes us always crave the highs of love. A certain dip might make us feel like there is no love left anymore or question the entire relationship.

Individuals in a relationship with high chemistry but low compatibility might not be able to have honest and authentic conversations. They might fear that the conversations will lead to emotional outbursts and make the relationship less stable. This leads to unmet needs, feeling unheard, misunderstood, and resentful, all while trying to have a great time. The relationship that was once a whirlwind of romance slowly starts to be punctuated by fights that seem to pop out of nowhere, angry tears, and suffering. Both individuals are unable to understand what is wrong and cannot seem to find any reason to stay or leave the relationship.

To question the relationship requires courage.

And Misha had mustered up all the courage that day. She really wanted to get her priorities straight and ask Rohit once and for all—is marriage on his mind or not? She doesn't want more trips to Bali but instead wants to be introduced to his family. The gifts and words do not cut it anymore for her. She wants time, commitment, and actions to match his words.

But what happened then? Where did all this courage disappear? Why is she now scrolling past beautiful Airbnb's instead of eating chocolate ice cream to soothe her heartbreak and crying to Anusha about how difficult it is? Why?

Multiple reasons.

1. *Misha is hooked to the potential*—From the moment Rohit met her, Misha saw glimpses of the potential he had. She has fallen in love with what they can be when they are finally together—not caring about what they are *now*. Misha is obsessed with the version of Rohit she has seen on holidays—the Rohit who has all the time in the world of her, who is vulnerable with her, promises to give her everything she wants, and tells her she is the one for him. She is not ready to accept the reality of how Rohit is actually not the person he says he is. She believes in the potential and would rather wait for Rohit to show up consistently one day instead of choosing her needs and doing what needs to be done in order to prioritise them.

But prioritising needs doesn't come naturally to her. When Misha was five, they welcomed a baby brother. After five years of being everyone's center of attention, now Misha was left to be with her elder sister who was already seven years elder to her. Her elder sister and baby brother grew up to be rebels, always getting into trouble, but Misha, Misha was her parents' golden girl. In fact, she was the entire neighbourhood's golden girl. Misha was quiet, never threw any tantrums, and did all she could to make her parents' life easier. She had the feeling that her siblings almost resented her at times.

Misha knew from an early age that anything that doesn't align with her parents' beliefs and needs was not to be done. She wanted to be loved, to be chosen, and to be appreciated. So, she taught herself that pleasing someone was the only way to be loved and appreciated. Nobody likes a person who talks back or breaks the rules. So that's what Misha does. She lets the other person take the lead and doesn't see assertiveness as a quality that is likeable.

2. *Misha is afraid of being rejected and abandoned*— Misha believes that being assertive doesn't do much good, except to lose the love you can get by conforming. She knows that standing up for her needs will lead her to have a discussion with Rohit that will in turn make him feel uncomfortable. He could get angry or start disliking Misha—what if he doesn't want to give her what she needs? Conflict is something she keeps away from and to have a conflict with Rohit would mean that she would never be able to come back from it. She has seen Rohit angry and it is not a pleasant sight. Talking about what she wants puts both of them in an uncomfortable position—why do that when she can sail through with what she's got? Isn't it better to have love than not to have anything at all? Misha is afraid of his reaction and would rather numb her anxiety and needs through work and partying on the weekends. She tries hard to hide everything from Rohit. She doesn't want to come across as too strong or nagging and ultimately drive him away.

3. *Misha is struggling with hidden shame and guilt for demanding more*—Misha has always been the peacemaker, the mediator. She never starts fights and tries hard to not be near one. She would rather die than take sides and be assertive. Misha is always the one who helps her friend out, she is always available for anyone who needs her. There have been times when she has gone out of her way to help her friends and colleagues in need. She prioritises others around her and is proud of her trait, wearing it almost as a badge of honour.

And why not? Growing up, she rarely saw her mother

demand anything. At least never in front of her. She saw her Maasi though. Her mom would always discuss with others how Maasi could never really have a family because of how 'moohfat' (loud-mouthed) she was. Mom always believed that being cordial and patient is the way to sustain a family. And she doesn't disagree. After all, her mom is happily married for 40 years now whereas her Maasi has been divorced and remarried. Her Mom didn't have it easy though—having to be the eldest daughter-in-law in a household with five siblings wasn't easy. The sister-in-laws made life difficult for her and she was always either sobbing or slept without food on many nights, unable to bear the family issues. Her husband was busy trying to earn and feed the family and had no time for anything except to manage finances. Her Mom suffered so that she could give the kids the life she never had. And rightly so…Misha had a life her mother couldn't even imagine. Her mother was right—people who are demanding usually end up not being chosen.

Imagine you have always wanted a beautiful garden, full of exotic plants and flowers. You start by planning your garden meticulously. You decide what plants and flowers you would like and then proceed to buy seeds, get plant cuttings, etc. You tend your garden with love, time, and effort. The plants seem to be growing okay and look quite lovely. But as time passes, you see that there are many other flowers and leaves in that garden. Foliage that you don't quite recognise planting. But they look pretty nonetheless. So you shrug it off and let them grow. You assume they are just some seeds that were planted by birds. Soon, you can't see the flowers you planted anymore. Your garden has been hijacked by these *other* plants and flowers and now it feels like you are actually tending to someone else's garden. Would you let that happen to your garden?

This is exactly what happens to our beliefs. As children, our minds are fertile and empty, ready for seeds to be sown. We have endless possibilities on what we want to plant in that fertile soil. As time passes, beliefs start to grow. These beliefs are sometimes our own—we grow these beliefs as a direct result of our life experiences. At other times, some beliefs are gifted to us by society, our caregivers, our culture, and our peers. If we are not conscious, soon we start living a life entirely made up of someone's else belief system which is not truly ours.

Beliefs are nothing but thoughts that hold power over us. Some beliefs are empowering while others are not—those are called limiting beliefs. These beliefs hold us back. They limit us. They stunt our growth and deprive us of the full authentic experience that life has to offer.

'I am not made for a relationship.'

'I am bad at Math.'

'I am too young to be doing that.'

'I am too old to be doing that.'

'I don't deserve that.'

'I am not smart/talented/beautiful enough.'

Limiting beliefs are unconscious thoughts that we conjure to help us avoid any future pain or obstacle. The human mind is wired for safety. Our brains have one job—to keep us alive. Any slight sign of danger or failure, and the brain hates it. It doesn't know that going that route could be difficult but it would ultimately make us stronger in the process. It doesn't care. It just has one job, and it wants to do it well. Hence, limiting beliefs exist mostly as a coping mechanism. And weirdly, some of these limiting beliefs are not even our own. They are just passed on from family to family, generation to generation, and society to society.

If we are not picky about what we allow to grow in our garden, we might be soon tending to someone else's garden. Similarly, if we do not sift through and question all of our beliefs, we might have more beliefs that limit us instead of empowering us. The limiting beliefs might unconsciously make us live someone else's life rather than truly our own.

Could Misha be limited by the beliefs she holds about marriage and relationships? Is she living a life that is not authentically her own, but a life overshadowed by the women in her family and their beliefs?

Our brain is always planning a happy ending for us. For Misha, acknowledging and choosing her needs means that she might have to let go of this relationship with Rohit. Choosing to believe that one can vocalise their needs and be assertive means that she would need to set boundaries and prioritise herself, which might result in her losing friends or losing people who are actually close to her. What if they do not like her the same way? The mind, in order to protect her from the pain of rejection and discomfort of trying something new, has conjured certain beliefs like '*it is better to be a giver than to be a taker*', '*people who are assertive are not liked*', and '*silence is the only way to happiness*' amongst many others. And many of these limiting beliefs might in turn be clouding her judgment, rendering her incapable of identifying her true needs.

In order to live an authentic life, it is important to uncover our hidden, limiting beliefs. And how do we do that?

EXERCISE 3: RELATIONSHIP BELIEFS QUIZ

Instructions: Read each statement below and indicate whether you agree or disagree. Be honest with yourself and choose the response that best reflects your true feelings.

1. Love should always feel effortless and easy—Agree/Disagree
2. My partner should validate my worth and happiness—Agree/Disagree
3. Conflict is the sign of a failing relationship—Agree/Disagree
4. My partner should be able to know what I need without me having to tell them about it—Agree/Disagree
5. Being in a relationship proves that I am lovable—Agree/Disagree
6. I must sacrifice my needs if it keeps my partner happy—Agree/Disagree
7. If my partner truly loves me, they will change to meet my expectations—Agree/Disagree
8. I should always prioritise my relationship before anything else—Agree/Disagree
9. It's better to avoid confrontation in the present, issues can be solved later—Agree/Disagree

If you answered Agree to any, then you might have some limiting beliefs about how relationships should or should not be. Let's decode why each belief may be limiting:

1 Love should always feel effortless and easy.
   - This belief sets unrealistic expectations for relationships, as all partnerships encounter challenges and require active effort to maintain them. It may lead to disappointment and dissatisfaction when inevitable difficulties arise.
2. My partner should validate my worth and happiness.
   - Relying solely on external validation for self-worth can result in insecurity and dependence. It's important to cultivate self-validation and happiness independent of external sources.
3. Conflict is the sign of a failing relationship.
   - Viewing conflict as inherently negative can hinder healthy communication and problem-solving. Conflict can be an opportunity for growth and understanding if approached constructively.
4. My partner should be able to know what I need without me having to tell them about it.
   - Expecting mind-reading from a partner sets unrealistic standards and neglects the importance of open communication. Clearly expressing needs fosters understanding and connection.
5. Being in a relationship proves that I am lovable.
   - Linking self-worth to relationship status can lead to feelings of inadequacy and desperation. Embracing self-love and fulfillment outside of relationships is essential for overall well-being.
6. I must sacrifice my needs if it keeps my partner happy.
   - Prioritising a partner's needs over one's own can result in resentment and imbalance.Healthy

relationships require mutual respect for each other's needs and boundaries.

7. If my partner truly loves me, they will change to meet my expectations.
    - Placing expectations on a partner to change overlooks the importance of acceptance and compromise in relationships. It also denotes that we are hooked on potential and fantasy rather than accepting reality for what it is.
8. I should always prioritise my relationship before anything else.
    - Neglecting personal goals and aspirations for the sake of a relationship can lead to unfulfilled potential and resentment. Balancing personal growth with relationship commitments is crucial for long-term happiness.
9. It's better to avoid confrontation in the present, issues can be solved later.
    - Avoiding confrontation may lead to unresolved issues and emotional distance. Also indicates we might be holding onto temporary comfort rather than the sustainable health of the relationship. Healthy relationships require open and honest communication to address concerns and foster intimacy.

Here are some empowering beliefs to foster within for healthier relationships, regardless of where you are at in your life:

1. *Love is a journey of growth and mutual support, which may require effort but ultimately strengthens our bond.*

2. *I am worthy of love and happiness, regardless of external validation or relationship status.*
3. *Conflict in a relationship is an opportunity for understanding and growth, strengthening our connection in the process.*
4. *Clear communication and understanding are the keys to a fulfilling relationship, and I trust my partner to listen and support me when I express my needs.*
5. *I am complete and lovable on my own, and a relationship is an enhancement to my life, not a validation of my worth.*
6. *My needs are important and deserving of respect, and I am committed to finding a balance that honours both my partner and myself.*
7. *Acceptance and appreciation of each other's uniqueness enriches our relationship, and I embrace growth and change together.*
8. *I am capable of pursuing my personal goals and aspirations while nurturing a loving and supportive relationship.*
9. *Open and honest communication strengthens our connection, and I am confident in addressing any concerns or conflicts that arise.*
10. *Authentic connections are abundant, and the right relationship awaits me.*
11. *I am deserving of love, understanding, and acceptance from a partner who appreciates me for who I am.*

Chapter 2

Pretty Please

Understanding Coping Mechanisms in a Relationship

The couch today is occupied by a new client. He is visibly angry and maybe a bit nervous, his leg can't seem to stop shaking. The coffee in his left hand might be aggravating the jitteriness.

'They spoiled the coffee today. I mean, I go to this shop every day. I mean *every single day*. How can they just fuck it up?!'

'I can swear here, right?' he asks, looking at me.

I smile, 'Go on.'

'So yeah, I mean, they had just one job. How can they mess up a *basic* cappuccino?'

'When you saw they messed it up, what did you do?'

'I mean, what could I do?' He looks at me questioningly.

'Hmmm let's see…you could have pointed it out and gotten a replacement, maybe?'

'Eh, no, I didn't want to create a ruckus.'

I made a note.

'Also, talking about coffee, my help didn't come on

time today. Just randomly making excuses, man, the whole house was a mess. Maybe I should fire her. This is her second time—no third or maybe fourth. I hate the house being messy and so disorganised.'

'You like your routine and order, right? But tell me one thing, Harsh—what else is super messy in your life right now, apart from the wrong coffee order and your irregular maid?'

'Messy? Hmm, my work-life balance.'

'And?'

'My car seat, I guess…'

'And?'

'My marriage.'

'Can you give me more details?'

'Yeah, sure. I am 34, I have been married for seven years, no six years now, and I am out of love. Yep, that's what it is.'

'And what does "out of love" mean for you?'

'Hmmm, it means things are boring, listless. No sex, no excitement, no nothing. It's just the same old. I go to work, she goes to work, we come back and watch TV separately, and go to bed. We even sleep in different rooms now. It's a joke.'

'Do you have any kids, Harsh?'

'Kids? No. I am glad we don't have any, given the situation. Who wants to bring kids into this fucking stupid world anyway? My sister has a cutie though, and I am really fond of her. Also, Meera—my wife's name is Meera—her brother has twins. They are just the most adorable boys, they are six now!'

I smile and make another note.

'Harsh, could you tell me about a recent incident in your marriage that you feel is important for us to discuss today?'

'Mmm,' he laughs. 'There are many, but let me tell you this interesting one. It might give you some perspective. So, Meera is amazing at what she does, okay? She is in a great position now and she has worked super hard to get here, I agree. Now, she heads like a bunch of 50 people, okay? So, there was a party at Cyber Hub, and it had booze and stuff—of course, like all parties do. And now, get this, I am sitting at the same place this party is going on at. People walk in, and slowly the place is getting full. Meera also walks in and goes and sits down. I am just sitting there, I am with three of my good friends, and all my friends see Meera. They looked at me and asked why I was not calling her. And I *knew* it was a bad idea, but I didn't want to let them know our situation. So, I went up to her and tapped on her back. She startled at first and turned towards me.'

He paused and looked at me, 'Can you guess what happened?'

I shook my head.

'She just looked at me and said, "Oh."'

'What did you do then?' I urged him to continue.

'I told her "Oh? What does that mean?" She said, "No I meant what are you doing here?" So I pointed to the table where my friends were. They were of course all looking at us, so they waved. She waved back. And said again, "Oh, I see." And that sarcasm. That tone, I hate it. I shouldn't even have gone up to her. Such an inconsiderate woman, honestly.'

'And how did that make you feel?'

'I was so embarrassed.'

'Embarrassed...and that emotion surfaced because...?'

'Because I am her husband and I went up to her, but she did not respond naturally. She was reacting like she hates me, hates seeing me there. The entire office was watching, my friends were watching, she could have *at least* pretended. Faked a smile and a hug maybe. Chalo, just smile and walk up to my friends, say hello and all. This is classic Meera, never respecting anybody else's emotions except her own.'

Harsh is right. There is a part of his wife's reaction that makes him feel small and unwanted. It might tie back to the kind of discomfort both of them are already feeling in the marriage and given Harsh's apprehension at going up to speak to her, he might already have decided in his head that the conversation wasn't going to go well.

'So, I understand her reaction was very off-putting and embarrassing to you. Had you been in her place, what would you have done?' I ask.

'Mmm, I don't know,' he paused. 'Maybe I would have pretended. I would have smiled, gone to her friends, and chilled with them for a bit. I wouldn't have behaved so coldly for sure, but maybe she would never have come up to me in the first place.'

'Okay, you're saying you would have pretended and salvaged the situation had she come up to you?'

'Yep,' he nodded. 'That would be the right thing to do,' he said affirmatively.

It was becoming clearer. Most of Harsh's resentment in his marriage comes from the fact that he wants to cope with difficult situations by pleasing his way out of them, whereas his wife seems to have a completely different approach. His needs have been suppressed and perhaps even self-dismissed for a long time and he hates the fact that his wife isn't one to please her way out of a situation. That would make life so much easier for him.

People-pleasing behaviour is when you act a certain way to please other people. People-pleasing is exactly what it sounds like—when we act a certain way not for our own selves, but in order to please others. But honestly, it isn't as simple as it sounds. Mostly, it is pleasing people who matter to you, and more often than not, this habit also extends to people who don't really matter that much. Let's understand this behaviour better with some examples.

> Someone: Hey can you please pick up the book I needed from the library?
>
> You (in your mind): I have that favourite program on TV at 4, and the library is so far, I don't feel like driving at all.
>
> You (out loud): Yes sure, why not? In fact, I would love to. I was thinking I would go that side anyway.
>
> BOOM. People-pleasing.
>
> You: We are eating pizza today, right? As we discussed yesterday?
>
> Partner: Yes, I would like that too. We haven't had it for so long. But you know what would be nicer? Having hot chocolate and ice cream.
>
> You (out loud): I thought I wouldn't do sugar today but...what the hell, sure.
>
> You (in your mind): I really want to watch a movie tonight, I have finally got the day off.

The phone rings. You see it's your friend who chats for hours and you don't seem to have the headspace for chatting now. But of course, you answer. She has invited you for her kid's birthday and you can't say no; even if it is a short notice, you have other plans and you are tired. You end up 'promising' her you will be there and spend the rest of the time planning the perfect gift.

People pleasing is a coping mechanism.

When you agree to drive an extra 10 km to go to the library, and additionally lie about your intentions, you actually want acceptance, gratitude, and reciprocation in return.

When you agree to eat that ice-cream but later feel really guilty and snap at your partner for no reason, it is your inability to accept your needs and communicate them. But instead, you are blinded by your belief that *they* should have known, or *they* should have cared.

When you agree to go to the birthday party, you are not comfortable setting boundaries—that concept feels alien to you. You cannot stand the discomfort of what would follow if you didn't go, even in your thoughts, let alone physically. You consider going an obligation and keep your word. But later, when that same friend calls, you make excuses for not picking up the phone. In reality, you don't know how to escape long conversations if you don't want to have them, except to just put your phone on silent.

Our friend Harsh here is no different. In fact, he has been a prisoner of people-pleasing for a long time now. He blames his marriage and his wife because that is easier than blaming himself.

Let's understand why people-pleasing is a coping mechanism.

As kids, we have limited control over our environment—no say, no power, no control. We are dependent on our environment for even the basic requirements of food, shelter, and care. As we grow up, we realise that our basic survival depends upon our caregivers. That means if our caregivers are happy, we get the best out of them. If they are not, if they are worried, stressed, angry, or unhappy, it reflects on how they treat us. Well, most of the times. So we feel responsible for *their* emotions. We try hard to keep them happy. But why? Why do we try to bear such a heavy load on our tiny shoulders?

Well, most adult people-pleasers start out as parent-pleasers.

Parents who are emotionally unavailable for their children, who are too preoccupied with their lives, have a horrible temper or erratic moods, or yet others who might look at their children as a medium to fulfill their own unfulfilled dreams all contribute to why a child might people-please.

Children are like sponges while growing up. They are born with a clean slate. They start observing and making sense of the world beginning with their immediate environment. If they are constantly subjected to situations where they are left to make sense of the world alone, they use whatever limited understanding they have to take themselves out of discomfort. One of the ways they tend to do this is through people-pleasing. If they are guided with clear communication and spoken to with understanding, and not dismissed or invalidated, they make sense of the world more securely and confidently, understanding situations and perspectives that they might not have grasped alone. This communication and safety leads to them feeling assured and supported and allows them to navigate the world better later.

Interestingly, by the age of 7, most beliefs, habits, and patterns of behaviour are already developed. So if by that age we do not receive that kind of environmental safety or guidance, we subconsciously act out of our childhood beliefs and react to situations with the coping mechanisms we developed as kids.

However, it is important not to confuse people-pleasing with kindness. Nor with altruism. When we are kind or display altruistic behaviour, we do not feel any resentment for not having our expectations met later even though we are kind to others. If you feel that you have done something for a person and don't think about it for hours later, that's kindness. If on the other hand, you go out of your way to do something for a person and only end up with feelings of resentment for not being acknowledged, being used, and no validation from them etc., you might *not* be acting out of sheer kindness or altruism. Instead, you may be falling victim to wanting to be seen as a 'good' person.

Here is a list of questions that I asked Harsh, that can help us understand our people-pleasing tendencies:

- Do you have a difficult time saying 'no'?
- Do you feel that doing things for others will earn their approval and make them like you?
- Are you often telling people you're sorry?
- Do you frequently feel drained?
- Do you neglect your own needs to do things for others?

- Do you find it easier to agree with people instead of expressing your own opinion?
- Are you always thinking about what other people might think?
- Do you feel guilty when you tell people 'no'?
- Do you fear that turning people down will make them think you are mean or selfish?
- Do you agree to things you don't like or do things you don't want to do?

Harsh said yes to more than 70% of these questions. So I asked him, 'Would you consider yourself a person who thinks more about others than yourself?'

'Yes, absolutely,' he agreed. 'But what is the point? I always thought of Meera, did whatever was already required even without her asking, always tried so hard, but I guess it was a mistake.'

I nod. Maybe.

'You know Harsh, when we are preoccupied with focusing on someone we love and care about, it is easy to put our own needs on the back burner. That takes a hit on the relationship. A relationship thrives when you give and also receive in return.'

Sometimes we are so preoccupied with giving, that we do not know *how* to receive. We do not know what we want and can't seem to not feel guilty for wanting. So we go back to what we know best—giving—in the hopes that one day we will get something back in return. This causes a lot of resentment in an individual. How can we expect to get what we want when we can't even acknowledge our needs and accept them first?

'In order to reclaim your marriage and feel better within, I suggest you start by speaking your mind. It might take you a while to get a hang of it and it might be uncomfortable—like really uncomfortable at first. But I suggest you sit with the discomfort and do it anyway. You don't have to agree to a situation you can't make sense of. You can speak up when it doesn't serve you.

'For example,' I point at his coffee mug, 'let's start with the next time you order coffee. If they mess it up, can you walk up to them and talk about how you would prefer it instead of walking out with a cup of coffee that you don't like?'

He smiles. 'Maybe.'

'You can try, right?' I nudge.

'"Yep, I can *try*," he says after a longish pause. 'But you know what, I feel like a fool. I feel like I can't even talk to a barista. What kind of a person am I?'

'A person who has been in fawn mode for way too long now.'

'Fawn mode? What is that?'

'Remember we spoke about how a child, if exposed to erratic moods or uncertain situations, might be prone to hyper-vigilance and people pleasing?'

He nods.

'Do you remember someone in your surrounding as a child who might fit that image?' He pauses. 'I…' he hesitates.

'Go on.'

'I, I mean, yes, my Dadu (grandfather) was like that. I mean not in a negative way. He was a man of power. Everyone respected him, everyone was scared of him. He has a steel business, so he was constantly under stress, I guess. And the entire house revolved around him. His food, his sleep, his clothes. And of course, my dad and my grandma, and later my mom as well all made their routines around him. He had a terrible terrible temper, you know.'

He looked at me.

'Do you remember something about his anger? Would you like to share?'

'It is a silly thing I guess, but I remember this very clearly. 2-4 in the afternoon was Dadu's sleep time. I used to come home from school at that time, and I was also asked to sleep immediately after school. During that time, there was not a single utensil that clanged or a leaf that rustled, everything would be super quiet. Like, eerily quiet. For the longest time, this is what I thought everybody's houses looked like in the afternoons,' he scoffed.

'So, I would usually sleep—I was a very obedient child—but that day, I had won a trophy in chess at school. And I was so happy, so happy that I danced around the house. My mom and Dadi-ma were happy as well, but they kept on begging me to quiet down and sleep. And I wanted Dadu to know this. Dadu had a penchant for chess as well. I ignored them and went to Dadu's room, to call him. He was a huge man and was snoring. I shook him, and when he didn't wake up I called his name. He still didn't wake up, so I grabbed the radio from the shelf, cranked it to the highest volume and put it to his ear. That was my mechanism to wake him up,' he laughed.

'And? What happened then? He woke up?'

'Oh, he woke up alright. He grabbed me by the hair and gave me the slaps of a lifetime. He then took me by the collar and took me to the courtyard and slapped me again. All this while I was wanting to tell him I won the trophy, my grandma and mom were crying in a corner, begging him to stop. He didn't just stop at slapping me though, he took the trophy and smashed it to the ground. That was the beginning and end of my trophy-winning era. Never another prize after that.'

He seems to be in thought. After a short pause, he says, 'But, I would have gotten that angry too.'

'Really?' I ask him. 'That angry? To thrash and hurt a child?'

'Maybe not.' He pauses again. 'Not that mad type of anger. But you know what? It wasn't his slaps that hurt me, not even the trophy smashing. That did hurt more than the slaps, but then he didn't speak to me for a whole month.'

Hmm, I nodded. A child—merely 10 years of age—being subjected to so much rage and then the silent-treatment. He was bound to fawn as a result.

'How was your relationship with your Dadu after that incident?'

'It was alright, I guess. But I knew now to always be in his good books, because who the hell wants to be slapped like that? Dadu always loved me though. There was never a doubt about that.'

'And would you say you were overly careful about your behaviour after that incident?'

'Hmm, yes. I would always be calculated. Also, I didn't want to hurt anyone else. My grandmother and mother were hurt after that incident. I understood that shouldn't be done in any way ever again.'

'Harsh, our minds are a bit like superheroes, ready

to protect us when we feel scared or in danger. When something scary or bad happens, our superhero mind activates different coping mechanisms to keep us safe. These responses are called stress responses.

'The stress response is the body's natural reaction to a perceived threat or challenge. When we encounter a stressful situation, our bodies activate the "fight-or-flight" response, which triggers a series of physiological changes that prepare us to either confront the threat or run away from it.'

Here are some common stress responses:

1. **Increased heart rate and blood pressure:** The body's cardiovascular system responds to stress by increasing heart rate and blood pressure to provide more oxygen and nutrients to the muscles.
2. **Rapid breathing:** The respiratory system responds to stress by increasing the breathing rate to bring in more oxygen.
3. **Muscle tension:** The musculoskeletal system responds to stress by tensing up muscles to prepare for action.
4. **Dilated pupils:** The eyes respond to stress by dilating pupils to allow more light in, improving vision in low-light conditions.
5. **Increased sweating:** The skin responds to stress by producing more sweat to help regulate body temperature.
6. **Release of stress hormones:** The endocrine system responds to stress by releasing stress hormones like cortisol and adrenaline, which trigger the "fight-or-flight" response.

These responses are designed to help us respond to a stressful situation quickly and effectively. However, prolonged or chronic stress can have negative effects on our physical and mental health. Understanding and managing our stress responses can help us cope with stress more effectively and improve our overall well-being.

When we are exposed to hyper-stressful situations, where a person's emotional distress from an event overwhelms their capacity to emotionally digest it, it can result in trauma. Trauma can be classified into broadly two categories: Overt and Covert Trauma.

Overt Trauma: This type of trauma arises from clearly identifiable and often extreme events, such as physical abuse, accidents, natural disasters, or violent assaults. These events are explicit and can be directly linked to the traumatic response in an individual.

Covert Trauma: This type of trauma is less obvious and stems from subtle, insidious experiences. Examples include emotional neglect, chronic criticism, or living in a persistently unsafe environment. Covert trauma may not have a single, identifiable event at its source, but accumulates over time, leading to significant psychological distress.

Trauma can significantly alter your brain, impacting everything from your decision-making process to your immediate, subconscious reactions to your environment.

A 2006 NIH study (Bremner, J. D. (2006). *Traumatic Stress: Effects on the Brain. Dialogues in Clinical Neuroscience*) highlights that trauma primarily impacts three key brain regions: the amygdala, the hippocampus, and the prefrontal cortex. The amygdala, your emotional and instinctual center, goes into overdrive during trauma reminders, reacting as if the trauma is happening again. The prefrontal cortex, which helps regulate emotions and impulses, becomes suppressed, making it harder to control fear and leaving you in a reactive state.

Additionally, trauma reduces activity in the hippocampus, which is crucial for distinguishing between past and present events. As a result, if we do not actively strive to understand and heal from past trauma, our brain struggles to differentiate between the actual traumatic event and its memory, perceiving triggers as active threats. This can dictate our behaviour in the form of different trauma responses.

Here are the 5F's, or what trauma responses look like in different situations:

1. **Flight response:** A person who is walking in the woods and sees a bear might experience a flight response, and their body might prepare them to run away from the bear.
2. **Freeze response:** Imagine a person who has a fear of public speaking is asked to give a speech in front of a large audience. They might experience a freeze response, and their body may feel paralysed or immobile.
3. **Fight response:** If a person is confronted by a physical attacker, they might experience a fight response, and their body may prepare them to defend themselves.
4. **Fawn response:** A person who is being bullied

might experience a fawn response and try to please the bully or appease them to avoid further harm. They may also try to make excuses or excessively to defuse the situation.

5. **Flop response:** A person who is under extreme stress might experience a flop response and become physically or mentally immobile. They may feel a sense of overwhelm and helplessness, leading to a state of collapse or mental dissociation, leading to numbness.

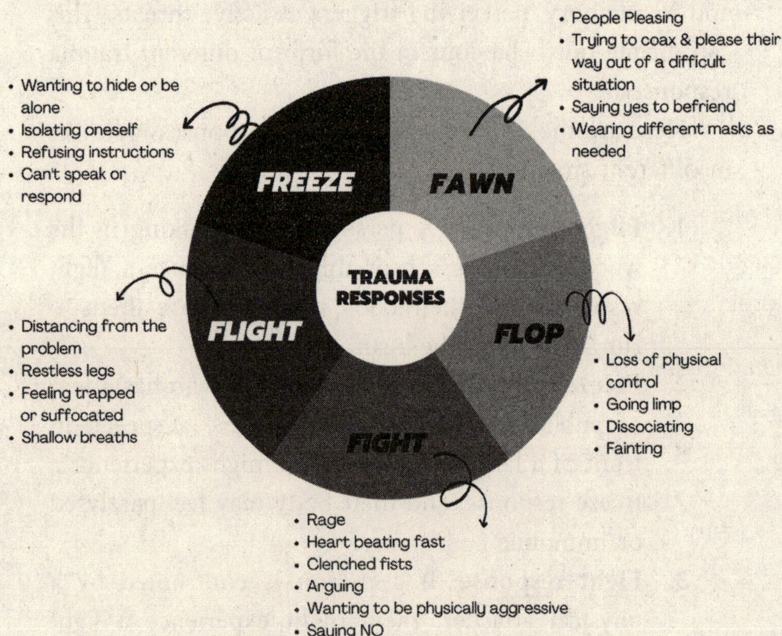

The different kinds of stress responses

The fawn response is like being a superhero peacemaker. When a child experiences something difficult or scary, they might unconsciously develop the habit of fawning to avoid confrontation or conflict. It's a way of trying to make everything okay by pleasing others and keeping the people around them happy.

Children don't choose these responses on purpose; their superhero mind just kicks in automatically to keep them safe. So, if a child has experienced situations where they have felt threatened or unsafe, they might start using the fawn response without even realising it. It becomes like a habit—a way to navigate the world and avoid anything that feels confrontational.

Fawning becomes a tool to escape situations that might feel too scary or confrontational. It's like putting on an invisible cloak to blend in and not draw attention to oneself. Kids might think, 'If I just agree with everyone and do what they want, maybe everything will be okay, and I won't have to deal with something bad happening.'

It's important to remember that trauma responses are normal reactions that our minds use to protect us. However, as we grow, it's helpful to recognise these responses and find healthier ways to cope with challenges.

People-pleasing as a trauma response manifests in various ways, often rooted in a person's experiences of past trauma or adverse events.

- **Over-Accommodating:** Individuals may go to great lengths to meet others' needs, even at the expense of their own well-being. This can include constantly saying yes, overcommitting, or neglecting personal boundaries.

- **Avoiding Conflict at All Costs:** A person may go to extreme lengths to avoid conflicts or disagreements, fearing that any form of disagreement could lead to rejection or abandonment. This may involve suppressing their own opinions or needs.
- **Seeking External Validation:** People-pleasers may excessively seek validation and approval from others, relying on external feedback to determine their self-worth. This stems from a fear of not being liked or accepted.
- **Constant Apologising:** Individuals may apologise excessively, even for trivial matters, as a way to prevent conflict or to avoid upsetting others. This behaviour is driven by a fear of being perceived as a burden or causing discomfort.
- **Neglecting Personal Needs:** People-pleasers often prioritise others' needs above their own, neglecting self-care and personal desires. This may lead to burnout and a diminished sense of self-worth.
- **Difficulty Saying 'No':** A person with this people-pleasing trait finds it challenging to say 'no' to requests or favours, even when it inconveniences them. They fear rejection or disappointing others.
- **Excessive Conformity:** People-pleasers may adopt the interests, opinions, or preferences of those around them to fit in and be accepted. This is a way to avoid standing out and facing potential criticism.
- **Hyper-Vigilance to Others' Emotions:** Individuals may become hyper-aware of others' emotions, constantly monitoring and adapting their behaviour

to ensure everyone around them is comfortable. This hyper-vigilance stems from a fear of causing distress.

- **Self-Blame and Guilt:** People-pleasers may internalise blame and guilt excessively, even when they are not at fault. This behaviour is often driven by a fear of being perceived as responsible for any negative outcomes.
- **Difficulty Receiving Compliments:** People-pleasers may struggle to accept compliments graciously, deflecting or downplaying positive feedback. This stems from a discomfort with being the center of positive attention.

Harsh nods, 'Makes sense.'

'So, no, you are not lesser for not being able to speak about the coffee, but you have been functioning in fawn mode for way too long now. It's time to be more conscious of your habits, but let's start small, okay?'

He nods. The timer dings.

'Our time today is over, Harsh. But I want to leave you with a small behavioral change that can help you feel more heard and seen, okay?

'Assertiveness is a key skill in managing fawn mechanisms, as it involves expressing yourself authentically and confidently without being overly passive or aggressive. Assertiveness lies between passivity (not expressing your needs) and aggression (expressing your needs at the expense of others). It involves communicating your thoughts, feelings, and needs in a clear, honest, and respectful manner. If we consciously start practicing assertiveness, it can help break the pattern of fawning and build healthier communication habits.

'Remind yourself that it is okay to have preferences and voicing them out is a key way to help people understand you, and in turn, live more authentically. You prefer coffee over tea, and that's okay. You prefer lattes—'

'I hate lattes,' he quips.

I smile, 'Americanos then?'

'Yeah, works.'

'So you prefer Americano's to latte's and that's completely fine. Just let the barista know. Sometimes you might have to repeat yourself but if that ensures a good experience, why not? Feel free to test your newfound awareness and get back to me by email if you want before our next session, okay?'

He nods.

The couch is empty, but it feels heavy. The energy of the child who was exposed to the rage of a caregiver he trusted and loved, which led him to develop people-pleasing tendencies so that he could navigate his surroundings better without ever getting hurt—physically and mentally—lingers around the room for a while after Harsh has left.

The coffee cup too remains by the side table. A reminder that healing is in the small things. I silently hope that his next coffee order gets messed up so that he can put his voice to use. It can be a truly liberating moment. I am excited to see him grow.

A couple of days later, as I mindlessly scroll through emails, a new email pops up. It is from Harsh, titled 'Coffee Fiasco'. His email looked like this:

Hi Kasturi,

I didn't expect to be writing this soon, but guess what, today morning I went out for my coffee run and encountered another fiasco. He gave me a cold brew instead of an Americano. I realised it immediately because it was so cold. I took a sip to confirm. It was a cold brew for sure. So I went up to him and asked him about it and he apologised and replaced my coffee immediately. It was actually so easy. TBH, I did contemplate drinking the cold brew and calling it a day, but then—why? I didn't want to drink a cold brew, right? So I did not.

It feels good to get the right coffee for sure. See you soon!

Cheers

'I am glad you encountered the bad barista.' I hit reply.

EXERCISE: IDENTIFY YOUR NATURAL STRESS RESPONSE

When faced with a conflict or confrontation, what is your immediate reaction?

a) Stand your ground and engage in arguments (fight)
b) Feel overwhelmed and want to escape the situation (flight)
c) Feel paralysed and unable to respond (freeze)
d) Attempt to please or appease others to avoid conflict (fawn)
e) Feel defeated and give up easily (flop)

How do you typically handle stressful situations at work or school?

a) Confront issues head-on and assertively address them (fight)
b) Avoid tasks or situations that cause stress (flight)
c) Feel unable to make decisions or take action (freeze)
d) Bend over backward to accommodate others' needs (fawn)
e) Feel resigned and demotivated, leading to procrastination (flop)

In social settings, how do you react when feeling uncomfortable or threatened?

a) Speak up and defend yourself or your beliefs (fight)
b) Find excuses to leave or distance yourself from the situation (flight)
c) Feel unable to express yourself or engage in conversation (freeze)
d) Go along with others' preferences even if it contradicts yours (fawn)
e) Withdraw and become passive or disengaged (flop)

When faced with criticism or negative feedback, how do you respond?

a) Counter with your own opinions or arguments (fight)
b) Ignore or downplay the feedback and avoid further discussion (flight)
c) Feel hurt or shut down emotionally (freeze)
d) Apologise excessively or try to make amends (fawn)
e) Feel defeated and lose motivation to improve (flop)

How do you handle conflicts or disagreements in your close relationships?

a) Engage in heated arguments or debates (fight)
b) Withdraw or avoid discussing sensitive topics (flight)
c) Shut down emotionally or become unresponsive (freeze)
d) Prioritise the other person's needs and feelings over your own (fawn)
e) Give in to the other person's demands to avoid conflict (flop)

Reflecting on past stressful experiences, which response pattern do you notice most frequently?

a) Reacting with aggression or assertiveness (fight)
b) Avoiding or escaping from stressful situations (flight)
c) Feeling paralysed or unable to take action (freeze)
d) Seeking approval or validation from others (fawn)
e) Giving up or feeling defeated easily (flop)

Based on your responses, you can determine which stress response pattern—fight, flight, freeze, fawn, or flop—aligns most closely with your typical reactions to stress.

Remember that it's normal to exhibit a combination of responses, but identifying your primary pattern can help you better understand your coping mechanisms and develop strategies for managing stress more effectively.

Regardless of which trauma response you default to, here are ways you can better cope and feel more in control of your situations:

1. **Fight Response (Aggression):** When experiencing the fight response, individuals may react with aggression due to heightened arousal of the sympathetic nervous system, triggered by perceived threats or challenges. This response is rooted in the instinctual need for self-preservation and protection. Here are some coping strategies (also refer to Chapter 9):
   - Practice deep breathing or mindfulness to calm yourself before reacting impulsively.
   - Use assertive communication techniques to express your needs and boundaries without aggression.
   - Engage in physical activities like exercise or sports to release pent-up energy and reduce aggression.
2. **Flight Response (Avoidance):** The flight response often arises from a fear of facing overwhelming situations or perceived threats. It stems from the instinct to avoid potential harm and seek safety. Psychological factors such as anxiety and past traumas can amplify this response. Here are some coping strategies:
   - Break tasks or situations into smaller, manageable steps to reduce feelings of overwhelm.
   - Challenge negative thoughts and beliefs that contribute to avoidance behaviours.
   - Set realistic goals and deadlines to gradually face feared situations or tasks.
   - Practice relaxation techniques such as meditation or progressive muscle relaxation to reduce anxiety.

3. **Freeze Response (Paralysis):** The freeze response involves a state of immobility and emotional shutdown, triggered by extreme stress or perceived danger. It's a survival mechanism rooted in the primitive brain, designed to protect from harm. Psychological factors such as trauma or learned helplessness can exacerbate this response. Here are some coping strategies:
   - Focus on grounding techniques such as deep breathing, visualisation, or sensory awareness to reconnect with the present moment.
   - Start with small, achievable tasks to regain a sense of control and momentum.
   - Challenge self-critical thoughts and practice self-compassion to reduce feelings of shame or inadequacy.
   - Engage in activities that promote self-expression and creativity, such as journaling, art, or music.
4. **Fawn Response (People-Pleasing):** The fawn response is characterised by a tendency to prioritise others' needs over one's own, often stemming from a fear of rejection or abandonment. It originates from a desire to maintain social connections and avoid conflict. Psychological factors such as low self-esteem or past relational patterns can contribute to this response. Here are some coping strategies:
   - Practice setting boundaries and saying 'no' assertively when necessary, even if it feels uncomfortable.
   - Validate your own feelings and needs, rather than prioritising others' approval or validation.

- Identify and challenge codependent patterns in relationships, such as overextending yourself to please others.
- Develop self-awareness and self-compassion to recognise when you're engaging in people-pleasing behaviours.

5. **Flop Response (Resignation):** The flop response involves a sense of resignation and defeat in the face of adversity or stress. It manifests as a lack of motivation or energy to confront challenges, often stemming from feelings of hopelessness or learned helplessness. Psychological factors such as chronic stress or prolonged exposure to adverse conditions can contribute to this response. Here are some coping strategies:
   - Practice self-compassion and challenge self-defeating thoughts that contribute to feelings of defeat.
   - Break tasks or goals into smaller, achievable steps to build confidence and motivation.
   - Engage in activities that bring joy or fulfillment, even if they seem small or insignificant.
   - Surround yourself with supportive and encouraging people who validate your worth and potential.

Remember that self-awareness is the biggest key to understanding your stress response and then slowly and gradually controlling them.

When we cultivate self-awareness, we become attuned to our thoughts, emotions, and bodily sensations, which are often the first indicators of stress. By paying attention to these internal cues, we gain insight into how we typically react to stressors.

With this awareness, we can identify patterns in our stress responses, such as recurring thoughts, physical tension, or emotional reactions. Understanding these patterns allows us to recognise when we're starting to feel stressed before it escalates into a full-blown reaction.

Once we're aware of our stress responses, we can begin to explore the underlying triggers and root causes behind them. This might involve reflecting on past experiences, identifying specific triggers, or seeking external support.

With time and practice, we can definitely learn to respond instead of simply reacting as a result of past unconscious trauma.

Chapter 3

Flags, Flags Everywhere!

The Red, The Green, The Beige

Ananya bites the pen end unconsciously as she looks at her phone. She is waiting for a message from Madhav. It's been an hour that he hasn't texted back and memories of all Instagram posts on her feed come back to her.

She doesn't know what to do. Madhav and she have been friends since seventh grade, when they were in math tuitions together. They have seen each other grow up and have had a similar journey of studies. Both have opted for Commerce and are in the same college. More than a relationship, they are friends. But recently, the vibe has changed. Things feel different. Ananya knows it. The way he speaks of his life and his future seems very intimate and vulnerable. Ananya opens up to him too…but not like she does with Vaidehi. It's always different with girlfriends, right? She reasons with herself.

But why is it then that an hour of not being texted back by Madhav makes her lose her mind? Maybe Vaidehi can help?

She calls her, and Vaidehi picks up in one ring. 'Why can't Madhav be like you?' laments Ananya.

'Why? How can he be like me anyway? Such a loser!'

Vaidehi has never liked Madhav. Now that Ananya is close to him, she can't stand him anymore. 'Why the hell would you say that?' Ananya snaps.

'Leave it, whatssup?'

'I want to talk about Madhav. He hasn't texted me back, we are supposed to catch a movie on Saturday.'

'Saturday? And what about the flea plan we had?'

'Flea plan?' Ananya had completely forgotten about the plan she had made with Vaidehi. 'We can go on Sunday, no?'

'But we made plans first and you said you were free,' Vaidehi sounds pissed. 'But babe, listen no…Madhav can't make it any other day yaar.'

'Okay, we can check on Sunday, if I am not doing anything we will go,' Vaidehi says flatly. 'But listen Ananya, Madhav is a huge red flag.'

'Why? Why do you always have bad things to say about him?'

'I just care for you as a friend, that's why. That guy is off…anyway, let me get back to you on Saturday about the Sunday plan, okay?'

'Okay,' Ananya hangs up. Vaidehi is of no help. Who else does she talk to about him? Vaidehi has always been a supporter until now. What if she is right? What if Madhav is a walking, talking red flag?

Doesn't text back? Red Flag. Doesn't communicate? Red Flag. Has a lot of friends? Red flag. Long hair, chiseled jaw? Red flag.

Tell me you are not on the Internet without telling me you are not on the Internet: 'What are red flags?'

Red flags—a buzzword of the internet dating world.

Although originally used in the military and armed forces to signal danger, red flags are now predominantly used to label or identify behaviours in a person that are problematic and you would want to steer clear of. And definitely not entangle yourself in a relationship with.

It is good to be familiar with the concept of red flags. It can sometimes act as a much-needed counter to your positivity bias, especially in the first few days or months of knowing a person. What is the positivity bias, you ask? Well, initially, as we are getting to know someone, we might be so blinded by only the good stuff that we end up completely negating or ignoring the bad or undesirable parts. We wear those rose-tinted glasses at the beginning of a new connection and keep them on as the honeymoon phase of a relationship begins. And while optimism and gratitude help build a relationship and continue with our partner later on if the going gets tough, a balance is required. Because more often than not, as the novelty wears off, we take our glasses off only to realise that there exist some significant differences that were previously unacknowledged, that we can perhaps still live with.

That being said, it is easy to go down the red-flag rabbit hole, so discernment is required, but more on that later.

Red flags describe general things that you need to be careful about in people. Here are a list of some general behaviours that can be marked as red flags, or behaviours to keep an eye out for:

- **Lack of Communication:** Difficulty in open and honest communication may indicate underlying issues. Relationships thrive on communication and if at the beginning of the connection, you are seeing signs of withdrawal in communication or inconsistent communication, chances are that you will have to work on this area really hard. If both people are low on communication, this might not be a deal-breaker for you yet, but if one of you can communicate while the other is completely shut down or not into expressing their thoughts and feelings, it can cause a mismatch.

- **Controlling Behaviour:** This refers to attempts at controlling or dominating decisions and actions within the relationship. It includes comments or direct control of what you are wearing, what you are eating, and maybe a constant monitoring of your whereabouts. Deciding for you, and not considering your opinion, commands, and orders are all part of this red flag. Whether you are someone who likes this or not, this is definitely a huge red flag.
- **Lack of Trust:** Persistent jealousy, suspicion, or constant need for reassurance can signal trust issues. Relationships are made stronger with trust, but trust builds with time and consistent actions. A big contributor to the lack of trust in people is previous bad experiences. When an individual doesn't make active effort to process past betrayals by either a lover, friend, or even family, it creates distrust in their minds. Consequently, they might constantly want to ensure that they will not be hurt this time. In such cases, being very clear

and upfront about needs and past experiences at the beginning of the relationship helps. But these past negative experiences cannot be used as an excuse to be constantly suspicious of our new connections. This is disrespectful to the other person and exhausting for the one who needs constant reassurance. Building trust is a two-way street and it is a process that needs time. But if a person, from the very beginning, is scared of being cheated on and wants constant reassurance even before a connection has turned into a fully-fledged relationship with commitment, the person might have unhealed past wounds and might not be ready for a relationship just yet.

- **Isolation:** This includes encouraging or experiencing isolation from friends and family and limiting social interactions. This is a big one, yet it happens very subtly in most cases. Isolation in a relationship refers to the deliberate act of either encouraging or experiencing a withdrawal from friends and family, thereby limiting essential social interactions. This red flag is marked by attempts to control and manipulate an individual's social sphere, often driven by a desire for dominance or to exert influence. This can manifest in discouraging social activities, creating conflicts with friends and family, or subtly undermining the value of external relationships. But of course, it is important to know that there is a difference between being introverted and isolation. Introverted behaviour is a personality trait involving a preference for solitude, and isolation behaviour involves intentionally distancing oneself from others. The major difference between the two is intention. Isolation is usually done with the intent of making it seem like the connection or our partner is the *only* support system and to ensure you are completely dependent on them.

- **Disregard for Boundaries:** This involves ignoring personal boundaries or pressuring someone to do things against their will. This is more common than we think. Examples include pressuring someone to get into a relationship even if the person has expressed their concern or boundaries, using threats or coercion to get their way like threatening to break up or going no-contact until they don't get their way, forcing a person to perform sexual acts they are not comfortable with, or sharing intimate details (experiences, secrets told in confidence) to others. In fact, boundaries can be bifurcated into 4 major areas:
  - **Physical Boundaries:** Invading personal space, unwanted physical contact, or ignoring explicit requests for physical distance.
  - **Emotional Boundaries:** A partner may overlook or dismiss the emotional limits set by the other, pushing for intimacy or discussing sensitive topics without consent.
  - **Privacy Boundaries:** Invading personal privacy, such as going through personal belongings or accessing private information without permission, reflects a blatant disregard for boundaries.

- ❒ **Time and Independence Boundaries:** Demanding excessive time, controlling one's schedule, or preventing independent activities can infringe on the boundaries set for personal freedom and individual pursuits.

- **Consistent Criticism:** Frequent negativity, criticism, or belittling behaviour. Consistent criticism might look like an ongoing cycle of frequent negative feedback, continual criticism, and belittling behaviour towards a partner. There is constant negativity that contributes to creating an environment where positive elements are overshadowed, contributing to an enduring sense of dissatisfaction and tension. Critical remarks become a defining feature of this pattern, where one person might be engaged in consistently pointing out perceived flaws, mistakes, or shortcomings in a condescending manner. Such behaviour can lead to heightened emotional distress, fostering an atmosphere of defensiveness and resentment within the relationship. This can have lasting effects on an individual's self-esteem, creating a toxic dynamic where the belittled partner may feel consistently invalidated and unappreciated, resulting in them trying to hide themselves. The other person feels a sense of superiority and power over their partner and feeds off these feelings—constantly complaining and enjoying the efforts put in by the partner to please them.
- **Emotional Unavailability:** A partner who is emotionally distant, unresponsive, or dismissive.

Emotions play a huge part in relationships. But then, some people are looking for everything else in a relationship except the emotional accountability aspect of it. This might look like not being ready for emotional displays but expecting physical intimacy, wanting loyalty but not ready to commit themselves, being dismissive of their partner's emotions, and not being able to provide any emotional support in the relationship. Imagine it like a person who is always up for parties but never available for slow nights or deeper talks. This friend is fun, might even have the right intentions, and definitely *feels* like a good friend, but they are actually only present to see the good side of you which slowly makes you wonder if they are only okay with the side that works for them and not the whole of you. That is the dynamic of an emotionally unavailable partner as well. An emotionally unavailable partner may struggle to provide comfort or understanding. This can result in feelings of isolation and frustration for the partner seeking emotional connection and support. After all, a relationship is not just about being witness to the fun after-party, but also being around to deal with the headaches afterward, no matter how non-glamorous it may sound or look like.

- **Drastic Mood Swings:** Extreme emotional highs and lows that impact the stability of the relationship. An indicator of a healthy relationship is the stability that comes with it. The stability of being with a partner who understands, accepts, and comforts us. A partner we can rely upon and feel supported by and in turn, also strive to support them. But imagine this: having a partner who is super elated, happy, and over the moon when you surprise them—they say the sweetest things and are ready to spend their lives with you—BUT when things do not go their way (maybe you forget their favourite colour), they question the entire relationship, threaten to leave, or even go no-contact for a few days or months. What? How would you feel? You might feel confused, blame yourself, feel guilty, and completely blindsided, not being able to figure out their behaviour. Even if both of you do reconcile, you might be very fearful or scared by what happened, resulting in you walking on eggshells to avoid upsetting your partner and in turn, hurting yourself and the relationship. The fluctuation between extreme highs and lows ends up contributing to an overall sense of instability within the relationship. Partners may find it challenging to predict and adapt to the emotional shifts, leading to communication breakdowns and difficulties in maintaining a steady and supportive connection.

- **Lack of Accountability:** Alright, now let's talk about another one—why refusing to take responsibility for actions, and blaming others for problems is red-flag behaviour. It might sound like a low-key red flag, but trust me, it's a game-changer. Picture this: someone messes up, but instead of saying 'My bad' they point fingers everywhere else. Imagine trying to fix things when all the other person's doing is pointing fingers. This indicates that the person is not willing to acknowledge their own contribution to problems and is more than comfortable dodging doing the work. Now, this lack of accountability is a sneaky but powerful red flag. If ignored, it can grow into a major problem. It's subtle, but it messes with trust, engenders defensiveness, and can leave you feeling unsupported. When there's no accountability, problems don't get solved, and everyone's stuck in a blame loop. Real growth and happiness in a relationship comes from tackling issues together, owning up, and finding solutions. So, if at any time you catch the blame game in action, pause and think: is this helping us grow or just keeping us stuck? It might be a small thing, but addressing it early can save you from a lot of headaches down the relationship road.

- **Financial Secrecy:** Imagine you are on your way to getting serious with your romantic partner and BAM, there is a PLOT TWIST. Suddenly you are exposed to hidden financial dealings or undisclosed debts your partner is under. This will likely bring forth a huge roadblock—a lack of transparency with finances. In serious relationships heading towards commitment, maintaining financial transparency is paramount. This is important because it establishes trust, aligns shared goals, and equips partners to navigate challenges collaboratively. Now, I understand that money talks might not be the most thrilling or romantic, but building a life together also comes with its fair share of challenges and is not exactly the rosiest thing ever. Building a life together involves a strong foundation of trust. Financial transparency acts as a key element in fostering trust, ensuring that both partners are on the same page when it comes to money matters. As relationships deepen, so do shared dreams and goals. Transparent discussions about finances create alignment in aspirations, paving the way for joint planning and achieving milestones together. By creating a safe space for open discussions about finances, couples foster an environment of unity and resilience. The quality of a long-term relationship is closely tied to how partners handle financial matters, making transparency an integral element in planning for a shared future.

- **Unresolved Conflicts:** This refers to repeatedly avoiding or failing to resolve conflicts, leading to ongoing tension. Most people are afraid of conflict and this might be an in-your-face red flag for most. But here is the thing—conflicts are not inherently a bad thing. *Unresolved* conflicts are. Conflicts, in and of themselves, are a natural and often unavoidable aspect of any relationship. They arise from differences in perspectives, needs, and expectations. The key lies in how these conflicts are addressed and resolved. Conflicts are not inherently bad because they can be catalysts for growth and understanding, providing opportunities for individuals to express their needs, share perspectives, and learn from each other. But when conflicts linger without resolution, they tend to fester, causing emotional distance and resentment. Lack of resolution can create an environment where issues resurface repeatedly, leading to a cycle of dissatisfaction and eroding the overall quality of the relationship. A non-accountable person contributes to the persistence of these unresolved conflicts, as they may avoid taking responsibility for their actions, allowing issues to linger. Similarly, a defensive individual can escalate conflicts, turning them into recurring battles rather than opportunities for resolution. It's crucial to recognise that the approach to conflicts matters immensely—from the tone used and the timing chosen to the art of articulation. Addressing conflicts with accountability, openness, and a willingness to find common ground is key to transforming what could be a potential strain into a catalyst for growth and understanding in a relationship.

- **Disrespect:** Consistent disrespect towards a partner's feelings, opinions, or values. Disrespect in a relationship can take various forms, and recognising these behaviours is crucial for maintaining a healthy partnership. Imagine a scenario where a couple is discussing plans for the weekend:
    - **Verbal Disrespect:** One partner dismisses the other's suggestion with a sarcastic remark, belittling their choice without considering their feelings.
    - **Invalidation of Feelings:** During a serious conversation, one partner trivialises the other's

concerns, suggesting they are overreacting or being too sensitive.

- **Ignoring or Stonewalling:** Instead of addressing an issue, one partner refuses to engage in the conversation, creating an emotional distance and shutting down communication.
- **Withholding Information:** Making a significant decision, such as planning a joint vacation, without consulting the partner or informing them beforehand.
- **Public Humiliation:** Criticising or making demeaning comments about the partner's choices or actions in front of friends or family.
- **Financial Disregard:** Making a major purchase without discussing it with the partner, disregarding their input or concerns about financial matters. Recognising these signs is crucial for addressing disrespect early on. Open communication, setting clear boundaries, and fostering a mutual understanding of feelings and perspectives are essential for maintaining a respectful and thriving relationship.

- **Abuse:** Any form of physical, verbal, or emotional abuse is a clear red flag. It is crucial to understand the different kinds of abuses that can occur.
    - **Physical Abuse:** Involves any use of force causing bodily harm, such as hitting, slapping, pushing, or any form of physical violence. This extends to actions like controlling physical movement, forcefully restraining, or any behaviour that threatens physical harm.

- **Verbal Abuse:** Encompasses the use of harsh or demeaning language, insults, name-calling, or the intentional infliction of emotional pain through words. This can include constant criticism, humiliation, or threats communicated verbally.
- **Emotional Abuse:** Involves non-physical behaviours that are intended to control, manipulate, or undermine the emotional well-being of a partner. This may include gaslighting, isolation, threats, or any behaviour that damages the partner's self-esteem and mental health.

It's important to note that while physical abuse is often easier to recognise due to its visible nature, emotional abuse can be sneakier and harder to identify. Emotional abuse can include tactics like manipulation, constant criticism, and undermining a person's self-worth, leaving no visible scars but causing deep emotional harm. It requires a heightened level of awareness to spot emotional abuse, emphasising the need for caution and a supportive environment for victims to come forward and seek help. Addressing any form of abuse promptly is crucial for the safety and well-being of individuals in a relationship.

- **Pattern of Deception or Frequent Inconsistencies:** Imagine you get a puzzle box from the store, and you are excited to complete this puzzle. You are invested in this activity. Mid-way you realise that some puzzle pieces are missing. You feel that way, but you are not quite sure. You can't seem to find some missing pieces, no matter how hard you try. But you keep trying to find them because you know there are still some pieces left and you wouldn't know until you get to the last piece. But this activity that was supposed to make you feel happy and light is now making you feel anxious, a bit distressed, and is keeping you confused. That is exactly what repeated dishonesty, lying, or hiding significant aspects of one's life in a relationship can do to the partner on the receiving end. When trust is compromised by a partner's repeated deception or the inability to maintain a coherent narrative, it creates a toxic environment that can have lasting effects on the relationship's health. Trust is the cornerstone of any successful partnership, and a persistent lack of it due to deceitful patterns can lead to emotional distress and hinder the overall well-being of the individuals involved. A healthy relationship is built on a foundation of honesty and reliability, and something to truly watch out for is a person who values honesty and feels safe and reliable.

- **Incompatible Values:** This is SUCH a big one. But a lot of us get too caught up in other things, and this factor is discussed, if at all, very late in the relationship. Picture this scenario: one person dreams of a nomadic lifestyle, exploring the world, while their partner envisions a settled life in a cozy town. These differing values can extend to various aspects like family, career, religion, or even the importance placed on certain virtues. When values misalign, it can create an ongoing source of tension, making it challenging for the relationship to flourish. Fundamental differences in values, goals, or life priorities lead to a lot of problems in a relationship. It often leads to a breakdown in communication as partners grapple with differing perspectives on fundamental aspects of life. This divergence in values can also trigger conflicts over life priorities, such as career aspirations or the importance of work-life balance, creating ongoing tension. Discrepancies in family planning preferences can be another source of strain, impacting the trajectory of the relationship. Additionally, clashes in religious or cultural values may cause daily friction, especially when navigating traditions and practices. Career ambitions and geographic preferences can introduce further challenges, as partners may struggle to find a compromise that satisfies both individuals. Lastly, financial disagreements stemming from differing values regarding spending habits and future planning can contribute to persistent disputes. So, it is a great idea to keep all of this in mind and not let just the dopamine and oxytocin do their job.

But something that is important for all of you to know: identifying red flags in a relationship is a subjective process that varies from person to person based on individual values, experiences, and preferences. What may be a red flag for one person might not raise the same concerns for another. It's like having a unique set of filters through which we interpret behaviours and actions.

This brings me to another kind of flag that is important to identify—Green Flags.

Just like red flags are behaviours to be discerning and cautious about, green flags are the go-ahead and desirable behaviours a person displays. This ensures health and sustainability in a relationship.

To navigate this, it becomes crucial to be attuned to your own green flags—the positive attributes or behaviours that align with your values and contribute to a healthy relationship. Knowing what you want is as essential as recognising what you don't want. It involves reflecting on your values, priorities, and the qualities that make a relationship fulfilling for you.

Understanding your green flags allows you to establish a positive framework for assessing potential partners. It helps you not only identify red flags but also actively seek and appreciate qualities that contribute to a strong, supportive, and fulfilling relationship. By being clear about your desires, you empower yourself to make choices that align with your goals.

Here are some green flags in an individual that can contribute greatly to a healthy sustainable relationship:

- **Good Communication:** A partner who actively listens, expresses themselves clearly, and engages in open, respectful communication.
- **Respect:** A partner who respects and values personal boundaries, creating a sense of autonomy and mutual respect, in turn contributing to a healthy balance between individuality and togetherness.
- **Support:** A partner who encourages and supports personal goals and aspirations, fostering an

environment of growth and self-discovery, allowing partners to thrive individually and collectively.

- **Alignment in Core Values and Life Goals:** This creates a foundation for shared experiences and a common vision for the future. It can be a key factor in reducing potential conflicts over fundamental aspects of life.
- **Emotional Intelligence:** A partner who demonstrates emotional intelligence, expressing empathy, understanding, and effective emotional regulation. Emotional intelligence can single-handedly foster emotional intimacy, creating a supportive atmosphere where both partners feel understood and valued.
- **Conflict Resolution:** The ability to address conflicts constructively, focusing on finding solutions rather than escalating disputes so that the connection can bloom into a relationship that can withstand challenges and grow stronger through adversity.
- **Shared Responsibilities:** Sharing of responsibilities, both in daily tasks and decision-making. A sense of equality and fairness in a partner contributes to a sense of partnership and prevents potential resentment, creating a balanced and collaborative relationship.

I hope this makes it easier for you to look for all the desirable behaviours you would want in a potential connection or partner. But this is life. And life is rarely this black and white, or in this case, red and green.

There is another kind of flag you must absolutely know about—Beige Flags.

Yes, you read that right. Beige flags are the in-betweens, these weird personality traits of your partner that sort of make you question their choices, but are not red enough to be complete deal-breakers. Think ketchup on everything, eating rice without dal, dipping cookies in water instead of milk, chai without ginger and elaichi, maybe owning just two pairs of underwear, putting up dog pictures on a dating profile as an icebreaker, etc. Or things like occasional lapses in communication or delayed responses that may indicate varying levels of engagement, slight misalignments in long-term goals or priorities that may require clarification, or even occasional misunderstandings or unclear communication, where both of you have created the safe space to clear such a misunderstanding or miscommunication when both of you are ready.

Beige flags started as a trend on social media, but I seem to like this otherwise as well. It indicates that a relationship is not only about the red or green flags, but also include oddities and quirks that we all need to adjust to as humans. We are not meant to be perfect, nor should we expect our partners to be. Our relationships are an ever-evolving, messy, and glorious ball of hopes, dreams, and emotions, so why not normalise some behaviours that we are not particularly a fan of but can try to accept and live with because there are so many other things we value and love in the bigger picture? Beige flags serve as gentle reminders in a relationship, teaching us to embrace fluidity and be comfortable with the nuances that come with human interactions.

They highlight that occasional peculiarities or small hiccups, perhaps some odd behaviour or less-than-perfect moments are inherent in any relationship. The essence lies in recognising that these subtleties don't necessarily define or jeopardise the overall quality of a good relationship. Instead, they provide opportunities for understanding, growth, and acceptance. Beige flags encourage us to navigate through the shades of complexity in relationships, fostering resilience, and emphasising that imperfections are a natural part of the intricate tapestry that makes each relationship unique. They teach us to be more forgiving, understanding, and appreciative of the journey, acknowledging that the occasional quirk or hiccup doesn't diminish the overall strength and beauty of a healthy and enduring connection.

'Hey, sorry for the delay, I fell asleep. Really tired after cricket practice.' Ananya's screen lights up to Madhav's text.

Ananya hasn't seen it yet. She is busy googling if Madhav is a red flag.

Do two beige flags cancel each other out? Only time will tell, I guess!

EXERCISE: SELF-ASSESSMENT OF YOUR CONNECTION OR RELATIONSHIP

This questionnaire is designed to help you gain insights into the dynamics of your relationship. By answering these yes, no, or maybe questions, you'll be able to evaluate whether your relationship exhibits green, red, or beige flags.

P.S.: This self-assessment is a tool for reflection and does not replace professional advice. Being honest in your responses will help.

How to score your answers:

- **Yes:** Assign 2 points for each 'Yes' response.
- **Maybe:** Assign 1 point for each 'Maybe' response.
- **No:** Assign 0 points for each 'No' response.

Relationship Assessment Questions:

- **Communication:**
    - a. Do you feel heard and understood by your partner?
    - b. Is there open and honest communication in your relationship?
    - c. Are disagreements handled constructively?
- **Trust:**
    - a. Do you trust your partner completely?
    - b. Have there been any breaches of trust in the relationship?
    - c. Do you feel secure in the relationship?
- **Shared Values:**
    - a. Do you and your partner share similar values and life goals?
    - b. Are there fundamental differences in your values or priorities?
    - c. Have you discussed long-term plans together?
- **Conflict Resolution:**
    - a. Are conflicts resolved in a healthy and respectful manner?
    - b. Do arguments escalate into hurtful or damaging behaviour?
    - c. Is there a pattern of avoiding conflict altogether?

- **Quality Time:**
  - a. Do you spend quality time together regularly?
  - b. Are there regular moments of emotional connection?
  - c. Do you engage in shared activities that bring joy?

Interpretation:

- **0-10 Points:** *Red Flags*—Significant concerns may be present, and immediate attention is advisable.
- **11-15 Points:** *Beige Flags*—Some subtle concerns or areas for improvement may exist. Addressing them proactively is recommended.
- **16-30 Points:** *Green Flags*—Your relationship appears to have positive aspects and is on a healthy track. Continued nurturing and communication are key for long-term success.

Chapter 4

Trauma Bonds

What They Are, How They Feel

'She is a doctor, you know? I just can't imagine how she is tolerating all of this yaar.'

Poonam's phone rings. She silences it without a second thought and continues to eavesdrop on the conversation happening behind her.

'…and when I was sitting there, you won't imagine, Shalini, her husband came home. I am drinking tea and she is also talking to me nicely, her child…my god the poor little girl, so cute, Mashallah, I'm sitting eating a cookie okay, and you know her house, is so beautiful so well-kept…'

'Yes, yes I know,' says Shalini. 'Go on, and her husband came and…' She urges her friend to go on.

'Haan, and her husband enters okay, he has his own key haan…and Manju's face drops, she stands up and rushes to get his tiffin and bag…I have met him a few times before so I said "Hi, kaise hai aap"…he barely looked at me…he was drunk! I am 110% sure.'

'Then, then…?'

The other woman pauses for a sip of coffee. 'Then kya, full-on Bollywood drama…Manju tells me "You please sit Nisha I am going to ask him what he wants to eat, he came a little early today." She rushes inside and I turn to the kid, just to talk to her. Meanwhile, the moment she went inside na, I heard raised voices, okay, I think he was shouting about something at her, I mean c'mon, there are guests, you just got home, couldn't have waited? I felt so awkward Shalini, so awkward…so I started talking to the kid. I asked her "What is the name of your doll, beta?" And you know what she said, Shalini? "Mummy-papa fighting again." Oh my god, can't even imagine how Manju is living with a drunkard ya.'

Shalini agrees.

Poonam is distracted by her phone gain. It's her husband. She contemplates picking up and then ignores it. She wants to hear what is happening to Manju.

'…but Manju also might be doing something wrong,' Poonam can hear Shalini say. 'Maybe she has an affair or something. College mein toh she had multiple boyfriends, remember? She used to be my roommate's close friend, she used to be in my room only mostly, always talking about boys. "Rahul gave me roses", "Shivam gave me chocolates", and distributing them around the hostel, such a show-off also.'

The other woman agrees. 'Might be, but still, you could tell that she is very unhappy. I don't know specifics but baapre, I am never going alone to her house again!'

'I will go with you,' Shalini chirps.

'Haan, next time we will go together.'

'Waise bhi, I hope she remains happy. Humara kya

hai, we are toh just concerned, na? She was a doctor. MBBS karke kaun chod deta hai after marriage? Now she is completely dependent on the husband also, so difficult it must be, haina?'

'Haan you are right, but leave the topic, let's order this garlic bread, will you share?' The two women continue with their conversation. Poonam is left alone with her thoughts.

She lifts her coffee to her lips, her cappuccino is now ice cold. Her phone rings again. It is her husband. She picks up, and without waiting for her to say hello, her husband shouts on the top of his voice, 'Where the fuck are you?'

Poonam goes red. She feels like everyone has heard his voice in the cafe. Quickly, she reduces the volume on her phone. He continues, 'Where the hell are you, why the fuck have you been ignoring my calls? Where are you, Poonam?'

'I am on my way, Rajeev, I will be home in an hour.'

'Come in half an hour, I am waiting.'

Poonam hangs up and stealthily looks around. Did they hear Rajeev's shouting? As she steals a glance around, she feels relieved. No body cares, nobody bothers. Everybody is in their own world. She signals for the bill.

Poonam leaves the café, dragging her small carry-on luggage with her.

Rajeev, of course, did not know about her plans, so she leaves her luggage in the security guard's room before going in.

The guard salutes her as he sees Poonam. 'Saheb is very angry, Madam, he was worried about you.'

Poonam smiles. 'I am here now, aren't I?'

'Yes yes, madam, why did you not take the car today, Madam? Saheb was very angry at Pandey as well.'

'Bas, Sunderji, I am keeping this bag here, Sushma will come to take it from you tomorrow morning okay?'

'Yes Madam, no problem,' Sunder, the guard, obliged.

Poonam drags her feet on the marbled stairs. The marble stairs were always spotless, the marble was of a special kind from Italy with some fancy protective coating. Rajeev was hugely particular about dirt. He would go bonkers over a tiny speck of dust. So funny, Poonam thinks to herself.

The door opens before she can open it. Rajeev stands there in a black silk robe, cigarette in hand and already drinking. He plants a kiss on her lips. 'Babe, I was worried…'

'I know, I should have picked up your phone earlier, I am sorry.'

'Don't be, jaaneman. You know what they say…Ishq ek Mir, bhari pathhar hai, Kab ye tujh na-tawan se utthta hai?'

Poonam smiles. 'That's deep,' she says flatly.

Rajeev has the entire dining table decorated, with candles and roses. Poonam just stands there, unable to comprehend her surroundings.

'I thought you might like this surprise, P,' he whispers in her ear. A shiver runs down her spine. She anticipates what is to follow. A night of intense, passionate, out-of-the-world sex. She would spread her legs, surrounded by the softness of rose petals, the dim glow from the candles, and Rajeev would be on top of her, hard and rough. They would be at it, like rabbits, and then end up gasping for breath and feeling parched.

Poonam shudders and closes her eyes, anxious and excited just at the thought.

A few hours later, she climbs down from the wooden table. Her legs feel jiggly. Her back hurts and so do her palms and knees. But most of all, she is thirsty. Is it normal to feel thirsty after this? She doesn't know. She has never felt this thirsty before. But now she does. And it scares her. She puts the water bottle to her lips.

'I loved…' Rajeev's voice against her ear startles her, and before she knows it, the bottle goes crashing to the floor. One tight slap lands her on the floor too, and miraculously she goes flying in another direction, missing the shards of glass that lie there.

As her body lies there, her mind wanders. The kitchen has always been her safe space. She has long comforted her siblings when her father used to have fights with her mother. Later, she used to sit near her mother as she tended to her bruises, sometimes with a hot potli and oil, at other times with haldi. She remembers her nanny, Shanta Maasi, trying to take care of her mother, but her mother, a proud woman, never let any help get between her and her husband. She never spoke badly about her father and always seemed to understand. Oh, how she wishes she could be like her mother. She tries, tries hard, but it is so difficult.

Rajeev was her choice. She chose him. She chose all of him, right? Marriage is hard. 'Marriage requires patience, and sacrifice,' her mother's words echoes in her ears.

Shanta Maasi had now been replaced by Sushma. While sweeping the shards of glass from the kitchen, Sushma furtively looks at Poonam, while Poonam casually moves around the kitchen, making coffee.

Why would anyone take it, you must be wondering. The right thing to do is to leave. Leave the relationship and walk out of the marriage. Why would anyone be with an abusive partner?

Let me explain. Have you heard of the Stockholm Syndrome? It's a psychological phenomenon that might sound a bit bizarre at first, but it's fascinating how our minds can respond in unexpected ways when faced with adversity.

Back in 1973, there was this wild bank robbery in Stockholm, Sweden. The robbers took hostages, and something extraordinary happened. Over time, the hostages started developing empathy and positive feelings toward their captors. Psychologists coined the term 'Stockholm Syndrome' to describe this peculiar bond that forms between captors and captives.

Stockholm Syndrome is like a psychological survival mechanism kicking in. When someone is held captive or faces prolonged stress, their brain can pull a bit of a Jedi mind trick on them.

1. Cognitive Dissonance: Imagine this—your brain doesn't like inconsistency. So, when captives experience both kindness and cruelty from their captors, it creates a mental conflict called cognitive dissonance. To cope, the brain starts rationalising the captor's behaviour, finding excuses or even identifying with their perspective.

2. Positive Reinforcement: Here's the twist—captors might throw in some crumbs of kindness. Maybe they share a sandwich or have a casual chat. These small, positive gestures create confusion in the captive's mind, and they start perceiving the captor as not entirely evil. It's like emotional ping-pong—cruelty one moment, kindness the next.

3. Emotional Connection: The brain loves connection. When hostages feel a semblance of understanding or empathy from their captors, they start forming an emotional connection. It's almost as if their brains are saying, 'Hey, maybe they're not so bad after all.' This connection becomes a coping strategy to survive the traumatic situation.

4. Self-Preservation: Now, bear with me here—Stockholm Syndrome isn't about the captives falling in love with their captors. It's a survival mechanism. By developing positive feelings, the captives might believe their chances of survival increase. In a twisted way, their brains are trying to make the best out of a bad situation.

Trauma Bonding in a relationship is similar to Stockholm Syndrome, though there are some differences. This concept was developed by psychologists Donald Dutton and Susan Painter (Dutton, Donald G.; Painter, Susan (1993). "Emotional Attachments in Abusive Relationships: A Test of Traumatic Bonding Theory". *Violence and Victims).* It is a complex psychological phenomenon that occurs when individuals form intense emotional connections with those who have subjected them to consistent abuse, mistreatment, or trauma. While Stockholm Syndrome typically unfolds in short-lived hostage scenarios, where captives form emotional connections with their captors as a survival mechanism in response to immediate threats, trauma bonding extends beyond hostage situations to encompass abusive relationships marked by consistent cycles of abuse and intermittent positive reinforcement. The duration, power dynamics, and the nature of survival differ between the two phenomena, with Stockholm Syndrome emerging as an acute response to physical threats and trauma bonding evolving as a coping strategy in the face of ongoing emotional or psychological abuse.

Interestingly, trauma bonding has distinct stages of growth and continuance. The diagram below can help you understand this better:

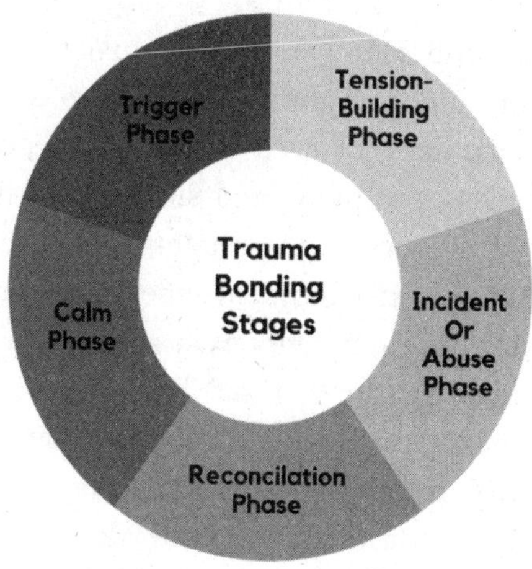

Trauma Bonding Stages

You would think that a person in a trauma bond doesn't really know that their situation is not ideal. That's not true. They do know. And they truly want to get out as well, but…the real deal here is the positive reinforcement that happens.

Often, people in trauma bonds find it difficult to seek help and remain in this web. Emotional dependency on the abuser, fear of abandonment, and low self-esteem can make it hard to consider leaving the toxic relationship. They may cling to hope that the abuser will change, making therapy seem unnecessary. Feelings of shame and isolation can deter them from reaching out for help, and over time, abusive behaviour can become normalised, further obscuring the need for intervention. Consequently, it often takes external support or a significant personal realisation for someone in a trauma bond to seek therapy and begin healing.

A trauma bond is interspersed with toxicity, abusiveness, manipulation, and gaslighting. Still, there are bursts of good moments, days, or even weeks, where everything is full of happiness, positivity, and sunshine. It is for those moments that the victim gets caught in the cycle—having witnessed those positive moments, they hang onto hope on bad days that those moments exist and maybe, someday, those days could last forever.

Picture this: just as you cautiously hang out your clothes to dry under the promising rays of the sun, suddenly, without warning, rain pours down, catching you off guard. This cycle is strikingly similar to a trauma bond. The initial positive experiences act as the sun, offering a glimmer of hope and warmth in the relationship. However, tension builds like rain clouds, and just when the storm seems inevitable, a moment of calm ensues—the sun peeks through, and the abuser exhibits kindness or remorse. This temporary relief lures you into a false sense of security. But, much like the unpredictable weather, the cycle repeats.

The deceptive nature of fleeting moments of calm and the repetitive, unpredictable patterns keep individuals emotionally hooked in a trauma bond.

Another very confusing aspect of trauma bonding is the almost out-of-the-world physical intimacy. A lot of individuals in trauma bonds experience high levels of sexual energy, which they haven't experienced anywhere else, and that makes them believe that there is so much love. But here is the real deal—in situations where emotional availability and connection are severely lacking, the physical connection becomes a compensatory avenue for seeking connection and closeness. The scarcity of emotional bonding amplifies the significance of physical intimacy as a facade for genuine emotional connection.

The heightened intensity and perceived satisfaction during sexual encounters within a trauma bond can be attributed to the scarcity of emotional attachment. The individual's desperate need for connection, coupled with emotional detachment, heightens the significance of physical closeness. This concentration, in turn, intensifies the sensory and emotional experience during intimate moments, creating an amplified perception of pleasure and connection. This illusion of safety and satisfaction emerges as a coping mechanism within the trauma bond.

The mind, yearning for connection and safety, clings to the moments of physical intimacy as the sole source of genuine connection. In these moments, the individuals involved experience a temporary illusion of closeness and fulfillment, reinforcing the cycle of the trauma bond.

It is essential to recognise that this heightened experience of physical intimacy within a trauma bond is a manifestation of emotional deprivation rather than an authentic, healthy connection.

While physical intimacy, attraction, and good sexual compatibility are important, a healthy and wholesome relationship extends far beyond just physical intimacy. While the intensity of physical connection within a trauma bond may temporarily mask emotional deficiencies, a sustainable, thriving relationship needs a multifaceted approach. Genuine safety, deep emotional connection, and mental intimacy form the bedrock of a fulfilling partnership.

A resilient relationship flourishes when individuals feel emotionally safe and connected. Emotional intimacy fosters a profound understanding, empathy, and shared vulnerability, cultivating a sense of security that goes beyond the (momentary) satisfaction derived from physical encounters.

Mental intimacy, intellectual connection, and shared values together with an environment where individuals feel safe without the pressure to perform physically in order to receive love and connection is what healthy bonding looks like. In contrast to the illusion of safety within a trauma bond, authentic safety within a healthy relationship allows individuals to express themselves without fear of judgment or rejection. It provides the space for emotional vulnerability and fosters a sense of security that goes beyond just the physical realm.

It is important to understand the various dimensions of intimacy as this not only strengthens the bond between partners but also fosters a sense of security, trust, and fulfillment.

- **Emotional Intimacy:** Emotional intimacy forms the cornerstone of a healthy relationship, involving the sharing of feelings, vulnerabilities, and life experiences. Partners create a safe space for open communication, empathy, and mutual understanding. This type of intimacy builds a profound emotional connection, fostering a sense of closeness and support.
- **Physical Intimacy:** Physical intimacy involves more than just sexual connection; it encompasses gestures of affection, touch, and closeness. Hugs, kisses, and non-sexual physical contact are crucial components that express love, care, and connection. A healthy relationship recognises the importance of both sexual and non-sexual physical touch.
- **Mental Intimacy:** Mental intimacy involves intellectual connection and shared thoughts. Engaging in meaningful conversations, discussing ideas, and respecting each other's perspectives contribute to mental intimacy. Partners feel intellectually stimulated and valued for their thoughts, fostering a deep sense of connection beyond the emotional and physical realms.
- **Spiritual Intimacy:** Spiritual intimacy goes beyond religious beliefs and involves a shared sense of purpose, values, and life goals. It's about aligning core beliefs, finding meaning together, and supporting each other's spiritual growth. This dimension of intimacy adds depth and purpose to the relationship.
- **Recreational Intimacy:** Enjoying shared activities and hobbies creates recreational intimacy. Whether

it's pursuing common interests or discovering new ones together, engaging in enjoyable pastimes strengthens the bond and creates lasting memories. Recreational intimacy fosters a sense of companionship and shared joy.

- **Conflict Intimacy:** Conflict intimacy refers to the ability to navigate disagreements and challenges constructively. In a healthy relationship, partners communicate openly during conflicts, seeking resolution without compromising their emotional connection. Managing conflicts together builds trust and resilience.
- **Creative Intimacy:** Creative intimacy involves exploring and expressing creativity together. Whether it's artistic endeavours, problem-solving, or simply brainstorming ideas, engaging in creative activities fosters a unique bond. Partners collaborate, inspire, and support each other's creative pursuits.
- **Adventurous Intimacy:** Sharing new experiences, adventures, and exploring the unknown contribute to adventurous intimacy. From travel to trying new activities, the shared sense of discovery creates excitement and strengthens the bond by creating a bank of shared memories.

Most of these levels of intimacy might not even be understood, expected, or ever experienced in a trauma bond, while a victim's lack of understanding and expectation from the relationship and oneself can result in several other behaviours that foster a confusing and very toxic environment.

Some behaviours that a victim in a trauma bond often tends to display are:

- **Justifying Abuse:** Rationalising or justifying the abuser's actions to maintain the illusion of connection. Poonam has not seen a stressed person act any differently. Her father was the same, and her understanding of anger is such. She knows the relationship is not great, but she also refuses to recognise it as full-blown abuse.
- **Isolation:** Withdrawing from friends and family as the trauma bond deepens, leading to increased dependency on the abuser. Poonam is isolated and has no immediate family she is close with. Rajeev is her only solace, and that doesn't help.
- **Self-Blame:** Internalising the blame for the abusive behaviour, fostering feelings of guilt and unworthiness. Poonam feels like she is too sensitive, she can be better, she can show up better, and that can help the way Rajeev is. She tries hard to be a good wife and she truly feels ashamed of wanting to leave. That thought is buried in a corner of her mind for another triggering time.
- **Fear of Abandonment:** A heightened fear of being abandoned or rejected, driving compliance with the abuser's demands. She has never been alone, what would she do without her marriage? She has no experience when it comes to work, what would she do?
- **Inability to Break Away:** Difficulty in disentangling from the relationship despite recognising its

toxicity. Poonam never saw her mother in a healthy marriage; in fact, she saw her mother being resilient and making excuses for her husband's poor behaviour. Poonam tries hard to be a good wife because she knows Rajeev's good side. She can't forget the times he went out of his way to surprise her on every birthday and anniversary, and she would like to let go of his volatile anger. In fact, he is super busy and stressed at work, so shouldn't home be his space? He shows a side to her that he doesn't show anyone else. And what of the fact that he chose her when he could get anyone else?

Trauma bonds, which are more common than we often realise, can weave a very complex web that makes it challenging to break free.

Recognising the signs early on and taking deliberate steps can be crucial in protecting oneself from the potentially harmful effects of such bonds. Here's a guide to understanding and navigating trauma bonds:

- **Cultivate Self-Awareness:**
  - ***Stay Mindful:*** Be attentive to the dynamics of the relationship and pay close attention to how it makes you feel. Mindfulness helps you recognise any unsettling patterns or emotions that may indicate a potential trauma bond.
- **Watch for Red Flags:**
  - ***Lovebombing Alert:*** Be cautious of lovebombing—an excessive display of affection

or attention early in the relationship. Genuine connections often develop gradually, so be wary of intense expressions of love or commitment too soon.

- ***Control and Abuse Indicators:*** Monitor for controlling behaviours and signs of an abusive personality. Observe how the person treats others, as it often mirrors how they may treat you over time.

- **Take It Slow:**
  - ***Gradual Progression:*** Resist the urge to rush the relationship. Healthy connections develop at a steady pace, allowing for a genuine understanding of each other. Taking it slow provides a clearer perspective on the relationship's dynamics.
- **Involve Support Networks:**
  - ***Seek Input from Others:*** Share your experiences with friends and family. A fresh perspective from those who care about your well-being can offer valuable insights. Be open to their observations and listen without defensiveness.
- **Trust Your Gut:**
  - ***Intuition Matters:*** Trust your instincts. If something feels off or uncomfortable, take it seriously. Your gut reactions can be powerful indicators of potential issues in the relationship. Don't dismiss these feelings.
- **Establish Boundaries:**
  - ***Define Personal Limits:*** Clearly communicate your boundaries and expectations. Healthy

relationships respect individual boundaries and setting them early on helps prevent the erosion of personal limits.

- **Educate Yourself:**
  - ***Understand Trauma Bonds:*** Knowledge is empowering. Educate yourself on the dynamics of trauma bonds. Recognising the patterns and behaviours associated with them can be helpful. Awareness is the first step towards breaking free.
- **Professional Guidance:**
  - ***Therapeutic Support:*** Consider seeking the guidance of a mental health professional. Therapy can provide a safe space to explore and understand the complexities of the relationship, offering tools for healing and breaking the trauma bond.

EXERCISE: RELATIONAL SAFETY ASSESSMENT

Understanding how safe and secure you feel in a relationship is essential, especially when dealing with complex situations like trauma bonds. A clear sign of a trauma bond is when you're caught in a constant state of feeling unsure, unstable, and walking on eggshells.

This exercise is like a friendly guide, helping you look closely at your relationship to see how safe and secure it truly is. We'll explore emotions, communication, and the overall vibe, giving you a simple but effective way to figure out if your relationship provides the comfort and safety you need, or if it reflects signs of a trauma bond.

Take this opportunity to reflect and discover whether your relationship is a source of security or if it's showing signs of being tangled up in the complexities of a trauma bond.

Note: This exercise involves self-reflection and honesty. Take your time to thoughtfully respond to each question.

Emotional Safety: *Rate your emotional safety on a scale of 1 to 10, with 1 being very unsafe and 10 being extremely safe. Reflect on specific instances that influenced your rating.*

- How do I feel when expressing my emotions in this relationship?
- Do I fear judgment or criticism when sharing vulnerable feelings?
- Does my partner actively listen and validate my emotions without dismissing them?

Communication Patterns: *List three recent communication instances. Analyse how effectively both partners conveyed their thoughts and feelings, and whether resolutions were reached.*

- Are communication channels open, respectful, and constructive?
- Do we discuss disagreements without resorting to blame or personal attacks?
- Is there room for compromise and understanding in our communication?

Trust and Transparency: *Reflect on a recent situation that required trust. Assess how trust was upheld or compromised and whether the issue was resolved openly.*

- Can I trust my partner with my thoughts, fears, and insecurities?

- Do we maintain transparency in our actions and decisions?
- Have there been instances of broken trust, and if so, were they addressed and resolved?

Physical Safety: *Evaluate your physical safety by noting any incidents of discomfort, fear, or violation of boundaries. Consider the impact on your overall sense of safety.*

- Do I feel physically safe in this relationship?
- Are there instances of physical intimidation or violence?
- Does my partner respect my personal boundaries?

Supportive Environment: *Identify a recent personal achievement or challenge. Evaluate the level of support received and whether it contributed positively to your well-being.*

- Does my partner support my goals and aspirations?
- Is there encouragement during challenging times?
- Are there instances of controlling behaviour or discouragement?

Consistency and Predictability: *Reflect on the past month. Assess whether there have been significant changes in behaviour, communication, or the overall atmosphere of the relationship.*

- Is there a sense of stability and predictability in the relationship?
- Are there unexpected and drastic mood swings or changes in behaviour?
- Do we have shared routines or rituals that contribute to stability?

Remember, your relationship should feel like a safe, supportive bond, not an erratic and unpredictable place filled with constant fighting or misunderstandings. If you feel uncomfortable or sense that something is wrong, please seek help. Start by speaking to a friend or trusted person if you're not ready to approach a counselor or therapist.

On the other hand, if you think things aren't too bad but some issues require discussion and working out, consider talking to your partner. A healthy relationship will always allow for free communication, acknowledgment of issues, and healthy discussions, even if solutions aren't found immediately. Both of you should be able to grow and learn in the relationship. While some misunderstandings and differences are natural, any form of abuse should never be discounted or normalised.

The dragging of wheels on the floor wakes Poonam from her daydream.

'Didi, this is the second time this week Sunder has given this luggage from his room. Is this something important?' Shanta asks, dragging the suitcase into the kitchen.

Poonam smiles. 'Yes, very.'

'Should I unpack and keep it then?'

'No no, just keep it in the closet for now, I might need it again.'

The wheels drag along the marbled floor, leaving a trail of soil and dust over Rajeev's spotless marbles. Poonam continues to sip her coffee, watching birds play in the garden.

Chapter 5

The Love Languages

Feeling Seen, Heard, and Loved

Pulkit is really on edge. They are moving in eight weeks and Chintan has blocked him, yet again. This is not done. Chintan is childish, he tells his mom, who sits there peeling oranges.

She rolls her eyes. 'I have told you that before, haven't I?'

'Mom, please, are you on my side or not?'

'I am on your side, that's why,' she resumes her peeling. Pulkit tries one more time. Nope, he is blocked.

Angry, he searches for Chintan's sister's contact. He proceeds to dial her number.

Chitra picks up after a weirdly long wait. She usually is responsive. Pulkit is pretty sure she is being told what to do by Chintan.

'Yes, bhaiya?'

'Chitra, where is Chintan?'

'Umm, Chintan is not here bhaiya.'

'Please don't do this Chitra. It's not funny, this is the second time in 10 days he is doing this, I don't really think I can do this, you know?'

'No, no, bhaiya, wait, give me one sec…So bhaiya, Chintan is really depressed, I think,' she whispers.

'Depressed? He was fine yesterday.' Pulkit is confused. When did Chintan become depressed? Chintan was this happy-go-lucky person. Someone who took life as it came and never one to really keep silent or not speak his mind. What was happening?

'Come meet him, he will be home.'

'I don't want to invade his space right now, Chitra.'

'No, he really needs you bhaiya.'

'Does he?'

'Why would he block me then?'

'You come and ask him only no. See you.'

Pulkit hangs up. His mother is staring at him.

'What happened then?' she asks. His mother loved Chintan, but of course, cared about Pulkit more. I mean a mother would always prioritise her child first, no?

Pulkit gets out of the house to drive over to Chintan's. If somebody had asked him a year ago if he saw himself living in with someone, he would laugh. For the longest time, Pulkit has not been the kind to focus on any relationship at all. A little flirting here and there, a bit of late-night chatting, and that's it. In fact, nobody in his professional circle knows about his orientation, though they might have guessed. Thirty-seven, successful, and still single. Why would that be, especially in India? Pulkit knows people talk, but that shouldn't be a reason to not live the way he wants. He has done this all his life—living life scared and playing it small, becoming almost inconspicuous and invisible because he didn't want to be different. But once he crossed that barrier, somehow organically, he felt free.

Not from a relationship perspective, though. He has never really cared about any long-term relationship. His career has been his focus.

Chintan has been a breath of fresh air in his life. He is extroverted, has the best taste in cocktails, and is ambitious. He has just the right kind of extraversion for Pulkit's taste—not too loud but always has the right conversation starters. Chintan was born in a pretty small place, had worked his way up, moved abroad for studies, and was now back to establish his own company. In fact, Pulkit was the one to suggest moving in, which was such a bold move even for Chintan. He was surprised, almost taken aback, but eventually agreed. Chintan wasn't ecstatic about it from the beginning. He had quite a lot of questions and worries but Pulkit knew it could all be managed. So, with a bit of reassurance, Chintan had agreed. But that was three months ago. The past two weeks had been a roller coaster. Probably the most difficult in their two-year-long relationship.

Pulkit parks his car under the usual tree and walks over to Chintan's place. He glances up at the balcony. Chintan usually always watches him come over when he is expecting him. The balcony is empty today, of course. Just the rose from their anniversary has bloomed into a mature tree with a few flowers here and there—something Chintan has managed to propagate after watching a video on YouTube.

The main door is ajar, so Pulkit walks in, knocking lightly first. Chitra is sitting in front of the TV, scrolling on her phone.

'Hey bhaiya, Chintan has gone out just now.'

'Gone out, meaning?'

'I don't know, he just left. You met him downstairs?'

'No, I didn't. You didn't tell him I was coming, did you?'

'Of course not.'

Chintan sees Pulkit parking in his usual spot. He backs away into the shade and furtively takes another drag of his cigarette. He knew Pulkit would come at some point. But this time he is not going to get the reassurance or convincing he's looking for. This won't work out between them. Chintan is sure of it.

As Chintan walks up the stairs, he takes long deep breaths. He is prepared to answer all of Pulkit's probable questions. He can hear Pulkit and Chitra talking. With another deep breath, he opens the door and walks inside. He is met with a weird silence, until Pulkit gets up and tries to hug him.

'I have been worried Chintan. What's—' he stops abruptly. 'Did you smoke?' Chintan backs away in disbelief and storms inside. Pulkit doesn't follow.

Chitra silently goes back to scrolling on her phone, but something inside her tells her that maybe she should leave and come back in a while. While she contemplates where to go, Chintan storms back into the room. He looks at her and then at Pulkit.

Chintan says, 'Of all the things you had to ask me or clarify, the only thing you cared about was whether I smoked or not? How pathetic! You couldn't even come after me to continue the conversation?'

Chitra pretends to be busy scrolling, her ears on the conversation.

Pulkit just looks at him, trying hard to control his anger. This is a man who has promised to not smoke anymore and instead of being apologetic about breaking his promise, here he is, with the audacity to question him about his behaviour instead.

'I am already here. What else do I need to do to prove that I want this sorted? I am not like you, blocking other people and running away from my problems. I show up.'

It is now Chintan's turn to remain silent. Chitra's phone rings. She quickly silences it. 'Spam,' she mutters, looking up.

Both men were staring at her as if she is the problem. 'Can you please leave, Chitra?' Chintan is irritated. 'Arrey, but where do I go?' Chitra rolls her eyes.

Pulkit stands up and asks Chintan to have a seat. 'Listen, I know a relationship is not easy, but we can talk it out no, Chintan?'

'*When*?' Chintan is obviously frustrated. 'When? We never meet during the week anymore. Whenever you are here all you want to do is just watch some show. We never go on dates or do anything fun anymore.' Chintan has not rehearsed this, but it somehow comes out like he has.

Pulkit sighs. 'I didn't know you had a problem with that. The fact that we spend time together is enough for me, and we do stuff—we cook together, I pick you up from work whenever I can, we clean together. These are good things, right? Fun even.'

'Yes, I'm not saying they aren't good, Pulkit. But all that you just described, that's homely stuff. What about the *fun* stuff? The *new* stuff? The *interesting* stuff? Where's the *spontaneity*?'

'We can figure out?'

'But this is not the kind of relationship I envisioned,' Chintan sighs. 'Please don't judge me right now,' he adds, as he fishes another cigarette from his back pocket and lights it.

The room is filled with smoke and heavy silence. Nobody speaks. Chitra clears her throat. Nobody bothers to say anything. She clears her throat again. Pulkit finally looks at her.

'Bhaiya, have you heard of Love Languages?' she asks tentatively. Chintan looks confused.

Chitra continues, 'No no, hear me out. Love languages are the different ways a person receives love and feels loved. It is a real concept. You know, for example, Pulkit bhai feels like he is showing love, but you feel unloved. So it's a bit like Pulkit bhai is speaking in Latin, and you don't understand Latin. Pulkit bhai feels he is telling you and showing you what he thinks and feels, but since you don't understand the language at all, you feel misunderstood and not cared for because the medium of communication is lost on you. Get it?'

Yes, Chitra is right. Love languages are a real and incredibly powerful concept for healthy relationships. Introduced by Gary Chapman in 1992, this concept should be as popular as the word love itself. *The Five Love Languages* explores the idea that people have distinct preferences in the way they express and interpret love.

Chapman identifies five primary love languages, each representing a distinct mode of emotional communication. These languages are:

- **Words of Affirmation:** Individuals who resonate with this language thrive on verbal expressions of love, compliments, and encouraging words.

- **Acts of Service:** For some, actions speak louder than words. Performing thoughtful gestures and acts of service conveys love in a profound way.
- **Receiving Gifts:** The language of giving and receiving gifts symbolises love for those who cherish tangible expressions of affection.
- **Quality Time:** Devoting undivided attention and spending quality time together is the primary love language for individuals who value this form of connection.
- **Physical Touch:** The language of physical touch involves expressing love through hugs, kisses, and other forms of physical closeness.

Chapman's concept of Love Languages suggests that understanding and aligning with your partner's preferred love language can enhance the quality and depth of a relationship. By identifying and speaking each other's love language, couples can build stronger connections, foster intimacy, and navigate the complexities of love more effectively.

While it is not neceassry to have the exact same love languages in order to maintain a relationship successfully, a recent study (Mostova O, Stolarski M, Matthews G (2022) 'I Love the Way You Love Me: Responding to Partner's Love Language Preferences Boosts Satisfaction in Romantic Heterosexual Couples.' *PLoS ONE* 17(6): e0269429) has found that partners with matching love languages experienced greater relationship and sexual satisfaction than partners with mismatched love languages. This research also found that men who reported greater empathy and perspective taking had a love language that better matched the language of their partner.

Let's talk about each of them in detail and understand how these are incorporated in real life.

WORDS OF AFFIRMATION: Individuals whose primary Love Language is Words of Affirmation find genuine and uplifting words to be the key to their hearts.

1. Verbal Expressions of Love: Simple yet heartfelt statements like 'I love you', 'You mean the world to me', or 'I appreciate you', hold profound significance for those who thrive on words of affirmation. These verbal expressions serve as affirmations of love and create a sense of security and warmth.
2. Encouragement and Support: Providing words of encouragement during challenging times, expressing belief in your partner's abilities, and offering positive reinforcement contribute to a strong foundation of support. Acknowledging achievements, both big and small, further reinforces love through verbal affirmation.
3. Compliments and Affectionate Words: Offering genuine compliments on your partner's appearance, character, or accomplishments fosters a positive atmosphere. Expressing affectionate words, such as 'You look amazing', or 'I'm proud of you', reinforces love and appreciation.
4. Love Notes and Messages: Leaving love notes, sending heartfelt messages, or sharing thoughtful texts throughout the day are powerful ways to maintain a connection. These gestures demonstrate

a consistent effort to communicate love and affection verbally.

5. <u>Affirming the Relationship:</u> Verbalising commitment, expressing gratitude for the relationship, and reaffirming the importance of your connection contribute to a sense of security. Regularly articulating your love and dedication helps build a strong emotional bond.

We can gain a deeper understanding of what we seek in love by being mindful of our triggers. For example, someone might be fine with handling all the household chores but could feel very distressed if they don't receive validation or reassurance from their partner. They might become upset when criticised. While many of us might not fully grasp how we feel loved, we can certainly understand our triggers and what upsets us. By identifying these triggers, we can then focus on their opposites—such as needing reassurance or feeling loved. This awareness can guide us toward better understanding and communicating our needs in relationships.

Therefore, while introducing you to the concept of Love Languages, I have also included potential triggers for each type. While these behaviours can be distressing for anyone, regardless of their love language, some people might be relatively unaffected by them while others can become highly distressed, feel unloved, and experience strain in the relationship. Understanding these triggers helps highlight how different individuals react to certain behaviours and why it's essential to recognise and address these reactions in a relationship.

What is distressing for an individual whose Love Language is Words of Affirmation? **Criticism or negative communication.**

Criticism involves conveying disapproval, judgment, or negative evaluations, which can have adverse effects on a partner's emotional well-being. Here are some examples of negative communication that can be detrimental:

- *Constant Fault-Finding*: 'You never do anything right', or 'You always mess things up'. Continuous fault-finding can create a pervasive sense of inadequacy and erode a person's self-esteem.
- *Personal Attacks*: 'You're lazy and irresponsible', or 'You're not good enough'. Personal attacks can lead to feelings of unworthiness and intensify emotional distress.
- *Disparaging Comments*: 'You're so annoying', or 'I don't know why I'm with someone like you'. Disparaging comments breed insecurity and contribute to a negative self-image.
- *Comparison to Others*: 'Why can't you be more like [someone else]?', or 'You're not as [positive trait] as [another person]'. Constant comparison can foster resentment and diminish a partner's sense of individuality.
- *Dismissive Language*: 'Your ideas are stupid', or 'You're overreacting'. Dismissive language belittles a partner's thoughts and feelings, hindering open communication.
- *Blame and Accusations*: 'This is all your fault', or 'You're the reason everything goes wrong'. Placing

blame can lead to defensiveness and escalate conflicts, causing emotional distress.

- *Lack of Encouragement*: Failing to provide positive reinforcement or encouragement. The absence of affirming words can leave a partner feeling unappreciated and undervalued.

When a partner consistently experiences criticism instead of affirming words, it can lead to emotional distress, a sense of inadequacy, and slowly damage the relationship. While constructive feedback and discussions about improvements are essential in relationships, constant criticism without balanced positive communication can be detrimental.

ACTS OF SERVICE: This Love Language involves tangible actions that demonstrate care, thoughtfulness, and a willingness to invest effort in making a partner's life easier or more enjoyable. For individuals who resonate with Acts of Service, these practical gestures might speak volumes about love and commitment.

1. Everyday Assistance: Performing daily tasks or chores without being asked, such as doing the dishes, taking out the trash, or handling household responsibilities.
2. Problem-Solving: Actively working to resolve challenges or issues that may be causing stress or inconvenience to a partner, showcasing a proactive approach to problem-solving.
3. Surprises and Thoughtful Gestures: Planning surprises, thoughtful acts, or unexpected treats to

bring joy and happiness, emphasising the effort put into creating positive experiences.

4. <u>Support in Times of Need</u>: Providing practical support during challenging times, such as offering help with work tasks, running errands, or offering a listening ear during times of stress.
5. <u>Acts of Kindness</u>: Random acts of kindness, like bringing a partner's favourite snack, making their favourite meal, or leaving sweet notes, showcasing thoughtfulness.
6. <u>Quality Time through Actions</u>: Spending quality time engaging in activities that a partner enjoys, whether it's a shared hobby, a walk together, or participating in activities that hold significance.
7. <u>Expressing Love through Service</u>: Demonstrating love through actions, such as helping with a project, fixing something that needs repair, or actively contributing to a partner's goals.

These actions go beyond mere tasks; they symbolise love, dedication, and a commitment to actively contributing to the well-being and happiness of their partner.

What is distressing for an individual whose Love Language is Acts of Service? **Neglect or lack of effort.**

Neglect entails a lack of engagement, indifference, or a failure to invest time and energy into the relationship. This may look like:

- *Neglecting Everyday Responsibilities*: Ignoring or consistently neglecting shared responsibilities, such as household chores, financial matters, or childcare duties.

- *Infrequent Check-Ins*: There's a noticeable drop in asking about each other's days, feelings, or well-being, indicating a lack of interest in maintaining emotional connection.
- *Avoidance of Problem-Solving*: Not engaging in problem-solving or avoiding discussions about challenges in the relationship, leading to a lack of effort in resolving issues.
- *Disregarding Special Occasions*: Forgetting important dates or occasions, and not making an effort to celebrate or acknowledge special moments that are meaningful to the partner.
- *Failure to Provide Emotional Support*: Neglecting to offer emotional support during challenging times, not actively listening, and not taking actions to alleviate emotional distress.
- *Ignoring Quality Time*: Neglecting shared activities, avoiding spending quality time together, and showing disinterest in participating in activities that hold significance for the partner.
- *Lack of Thoughtful Gestures*: Failing to engage in thoughtful gestures or surprises, and not putting in effort to create positive experiences or express affection.
- *Routine Monotony:* The relationship falls into a monotonous routine without any effort to introduce new activities, hobbies, or shared interests, causing boredom and dissatisfaction.

Neglect or a lack of effort in the relationship can lead to feelings of unappreciation, loneliness, and a sense of abandonment.

RECEIVING GIFTS: This language is about the emotional significance of thoughtfully chosen presents. For some individuals, the act of giving and receiving gifts is a powerful expression of love, care, and consideration.

1. Symbolic Gestures: Thoughtfully selected items that carry personal significance, such as a book by a favourite author, a piece of jewelry with sentimental value, or a cherished memento.
2. Occasional Surprises: Surprising a partner with unexpected gifts on special occasions or spontaneously, showing a willingness to invest time and effort in creating moments of joy.
3. Handmade or Personalised Items: Crafting handmade gifts or choosing personalised items that reflect the partner's interests, hobbies, or memories, adding a unique and meaningful touch.
4. Celebration of Milestones: Marking significant life events with meaningful gifts, such as anniversaries, birthdays, or achievements, to commemorate and celebrate the partner's journey.
5. Acts of Thoughtfulness: Small tokens of affection and gestures that convey love, such as a surprise delivery of a favourite snack, a handwritten note, or a bouquet, showcasing thoughtfulness.
6. Gifts of Time and Presence: Offering the gift of time and presence as a valuable present, such as planning a special date, organising quality time together, or creating memorable experiences.
7. Expression of Love through Material Items: Associating deep emotional meaning with material

possessions, where the gift itself becomes a symbol of love and connection between partners.

8. Appreciation for the Thought Behind the Gift: Placing importance on the thought and effort put into selecting a gift rather than the monetary value, valuing the emotional meaning behind the gesture.

Gifts can truly be a great way to show love, keeping the romance and consideration in a relationship alive while helping partners feel appreciated and valued.

What is distressing for an individual whose Love Language is Receiving Gifts? **A lack or absence of consideration.**

Lack of consideration, effort, or dismissing the partner's desire for meaningful gifts can be triggering, leading partners to feel unappreciated in the relationship. Examples are:

- *Forgetting Special Occasions*: Consistently forgetting important dates or occasions, such as birthdays or anniversaries, without making an effort to acknowledge or celebrate them.
- *Impersonal or Generic Gifts*: Giving gifts that lack personalisation or thought, such as generic items, without considering the partner's preferences, interests, or sentimental value.
- *Disregarding Partner's Wish List*: Ignoring or neglecting a partner's expressed desires or wish list, demonstrating a lack of consideration for their specific preferences and interests.
- *Indifference to Material Expressions of Love*: Demonstrating indifference to the emotional

significance of material expressions of love, downplaying the importance of thoughtful presents.

- *Ignoring Gift-Giving Opportunities*: Ignoring opportunities to express love through gift-giving, such as neglecting holidays or events that traditionally involve the exchange of presents.
- *Lack of Effort in Creating Memorable Moments*: Failing to invest time and effort in creating memorable moments through thoughtful surprises or gifts, contributes to a sense of emotional neglect.

Showing a lack of consideration in gift-giving can lead to feelings of emotional distance and a sense of the partner's needs being disregarded.

QUALITY TIME: Quality time is a Love Language that centers around the significance of undivided attention, shared experiences, and meaningful connection. Some individuals prioritise spending meaningful moments together, this is their way to deepen their emotional bonds more than anything else. Here is what quality time might look like:

1. <u>Undivided Attention</u>: Engaging in deep conversations without distractions, actively listening to each other, and making eye contact to convey full attention.
2. <u>Shared Activities</u>: Participating in activities that both partners enjoy, such as cooking together, hiking, playing games, or pursuing shared hobbies.
3. <u>Quality Conversations</u>: Taking the time to have meaningful and open conversations about feelings, dreams, and thoughts fosters emotional intimacy.

4. Creating Shared Memories: Planning and experiencing memorable events together, such as vacations, date nights, or special occasions, to create lasting memories.
5. Quality Time over Quantity: Prioritising meaningful moments over sheer quantity, emphasising the importance of creating valuable memories together.
6. Being Present in the Moment: Being fully present and engaged during shared activities, avoiding distractions like phones or other commitments.

The *quality* of the time spent, the depth of engagement, and the shared experiences contribute to a sense of emotional closeness and fulfillment within the relationship.

So what could be triggering for someone whose Love Language is Quality Time? **Distraction or lack of presence.**

When a partner is physically present but mentally or emotionally distant during shared moments or is completely absent when it comes to creating shared experiences, instead choosing solitary pursuits or prioritising time with someone else over the partner are situations that can be triggering for an individual who values Quality Time. Some examples:

- *Constant Digital Distraction:* Being consistently engrossed in digital devices, such as smartphones or laptops, during shared activities, dinners, or quality time together, leads to a lack of genuine connection.
- *Limited Engagement in Conversations:* Offering minimal input or engagement during conversations, displaying disinterest in meaningful discussions, and failing to contribute to emotional intimacy.

- *Frequent Interruptions:* Frequently interrupting shared moments with distractions or interruptions, preventing the development of a focused and connected environment.
- *Failure to Plan Meaningful Activities:* Neglecting to plan or participate in activities that hold significance for the partner, showing a lack of effort in creating shared experiences.
- *Preferring Solitary Pursuits*: Frequently choosing solitary activities over shared moments, demonstrating a preference for individual pursuits rather than fostering togetherness.
- *Disinterest in Quality Conversations*: Showing disinterest in engaging in quality conversations, avoiding discussions about feelings, dreams, or important aspects of the relationship.
- *Minimal Effort in Creating Shared Memories*: Making minimal effort to create shared memories through special occasions, events, or activities, leads to a lack of investment in building a history together.

Distraction or lack of presence can lead to feelings of loneliness, emotional detachment, and a sense of the partner not being fully engaged in the relationship.

PHYSICAL TOUCH: Lastly, what does Physical Touch as a Love Language look like? It emphasises the power of physical connection, affectionate gestures, and the comfort derived from physical contact. Individuals resonate with finding meaning and intimacy in tactile expressions of love. Physical Touch is not solely about sexual intimacy.

While it can include expressions of physical closeness in a romantic context, it encompasses a broader range of non-sexual tactile gestures that communicate love, care, and emotional connection.

1. Simple Gestures of Affection: Holding hands, hugging, kissing, or gentle touches on the arm or shoulder to convey love and connection.
2. Physical Presence: Sitting close together, cuddling, or physical proximity that provides a sense of warmth and comfort.
3. Affectionate Embraces: Expressing love through warm embraces, whether it's a bear hug, a tight squeeze, or a gentle embrace.
4. Intimate Moments: Sharing intimate moments that involve physical closeness, fosters a sense of emotional and physical connection.
5. Physical Affirmation: Offering physical gestures as a form of affirmation, such as a pat on the back, a reassuring touch, holding hands, maintaining physical contact while together, or a loving caress.
6. Playful Touch: Engaging in playful touches, like tickling, play-fighting, or other lighthearted physical interactions that create joy and laughter.
7. Non-Sexual Physical Intimacy: Enjoying physical intimacy that is non-sexual, such as a massage, holding hands during a walk, or simply lying together in quiet closeness.

And what could be potentially triggering for individuals whose primary love language is Physical Touch? **Physical distance.**

This entails a lack of affectionate gestures, physical connection, or intimacy in the relationship.

- *Avoidance of Physical Contact*: Consistently avoiding physical contact, such as refraining from holding hands, hugging, or engaging in other affectionate gestures.
- *Limited Affectionate Expressions*: Offering minimal or no expressions of physical affection, failing to convey warmth and connection through touch.
- *Emotional Detachment*: Being emotionally distant, leads to a lack of desire for physical closeness and creates a sense of isolation in the relationship.
- *Neglecting Intimate Moments*: Neglecting opportunities for intimate moments, avoiding activities that involve physical connection, or neglecting the importance of physical intimacy.
- *Absence of Reassuring Touch*: Failing to provide reassuring touches during moments of distress, such as not offering a comforting hand or a supportive embrace.

Now that you know what each Love Language looks like, you must be really curious about which one is yours. And though it is tempting to say that you need all (don't we all?), it is a good start to familiarise yourself with your PRIMARY Love Language and focus on that until you get a pretty good hang of it. It's tempting to desire all the love languages, but the key lies in uncovering your primary love language—the one that resonates with you most deeply.

How to Find Your Primary Love Language

- **Reflect on Triggers and Resonance:**
  After reading the descriptions above, reflect on various scenarios and past experiences. Take note of moments that triggered strong emotional responses or made you feel exceptionally loved. Consider which love language aligns most with these resonant experiences.
- **Look Inward and Reflect on Giving Love:**
  Turn your focus inward and reflect on how you naturally express love to others. Consider your actions and gestures in past relationships or current connections. How do you show affection? What specific expressions of love do you find yourself offering spontaneously? Often, the way we give love reflects our own desires for how we want to be loved. Identifying patterns in your giving can unveil your primary love language.
- **Take the Love Language Quiz:**
  Another effective method is taking the official Love Language Quiz by Gary Chapman. This comprehensive quiz provides a structured approach to understanding your Love Language. Answer thoughtfully and honestly a series of questions that explore your preferences in various scenarios. The quiz will then reveal your primary love language. You can take the quiz here: https://5lovelanguages.com/quizzes/love-language

Chitra sits on the swing staring at the skyline. This corner of the house has become her favourite spot. Larry, the Persian cat Chintan and Pulkit have adopted, agrees, as it sits on the rug nearby, purring softly to himself.

In the background, Pulkit and Chintan rush around—their housewarming party is today. 'You know, Chitra, Pulkit comes home at seven sharp, and we have a no-devices policy in place,' Chintan almost gloats. 'You know what that is, right?'

'Quality time,' Chitra rolls her eyes.

'And guess what else? Chintan now takes Larry's litter out, makes coffee for both of us, and even cooks dinner when I get home late. What's that, Chitra?' Pulkit quizzes her.

'Acts of service, bhaiya,' Chitra says and curses herself for not bringing her earphones. Both Pulkit and Chintan giggle like children, high fiving each other in the background.

'Chitra, we never thanked you,' both of them stand behind her with a bowl of chips and drinks in their hands. Chitra feels super awkward. She senses something emotional is about to come her way.

'Thank you, for always being there for us,' Pulkit says. 'And introducing us to things that actually helped us learn so many new perspectives, about love, relationships, and each other.'

'We thank you for being in our life,' both say in unison. There's a cheeky pause. 'What's that, Chitra?'

'Words of affirmation,' Chitra rolls her eyes, and tries hard not to smile.

EXERCISE: SORT YOUR LOVE LANGUAGES

Primary Love Language:

1. ______________________________

Secondary Love Languages:

2. ______________________________
3. ______________________________
4. ______________________________
5. ______________________________

Now let's discover expressive yet simple ways to communicate each Love Language. Below are 10 examples for each, providing insights on conveying your sentiments to your partner.

HOW TO INCORPORATE PHYSICAL TOUCH

1. Spontaneously give them a little back rub or back scratch.
2. Hold hands when you're out and about.
3. When you're sitting together, rest your hand on their hand or leg, or put your arm around their shoulder.
4. If you're having a serious conversation, hold their hand or softly rub their arm while you listen to them talking.
5. Even when you're rushing off somewhere, make a point to lay your hand on their back or give a quick peck on the cheek as you pass them.
6. Make a point of maintaining physical contact when you're in group settings.

7. Get to know their sexual desires well and prioritise them. Make a point to be the one to initiate sex every now and then. Even when you're not in the mood for sex, make sure to remind them that they're sexually desirable and wanted.
8. Rub their shoulders when they're stressed out.
9. Kiss them on places other than their lips, such as their cheek, forehead, collarbone, or back of the hand.
10. Run your fingers through their hair.

HOW TO INCORPORATE WORDS OF AFFIRMATION

(Take the help of these phrases or craft your own. But speak honestly and often.)

1. You are so special to me.
2. After all of this time, I'm still so crazy for you.
3. It really impressed me when you…
4. I couldn't have done without you.
5. You inspire me to….
6. Did I tell you how grateful I am that you are my partner?
7. You deserve all of the praise at work. I see how hard you've been working.
8. I just wanted to let you know I'm proud of you.
9. I really appreciate you when you do…
10. I am here if you need me. I'm always in your corner supporting you.

HOW TO INCORPORATE ACTS OF SERVICE

1. Pick up their favourite snack when shopping for groceries.

2. Fix breakfast to serve in bed before they wake up.
3. Randomly take them out to their favourite restaurant after a long day.
4. Put away their suitcase when they're tired after a work trip.
5. Book a massage during vacation so they can relax.
6. Take care of the family and give them the day off.
7. Do their preferred date activity, even if it's not your first choice.
8. Make the bed with clean sheets.
9. Complete a project they haven't had the time to do yet, like organising the drawers or cleaning out the fridge.
10. Preemptively buy toiletries or household items before supplies run out.

HOW TO INCORPORATE RECEIVING GIFTS

(*Common misconception:* Gifts have to be expensive/It's a materialistic need. No, it's up to you...people with this Love Language care more about the gesture and thoughtfulness rather than the cost of the gift. Time to get creative, then!)

1. Bring them their favourite flowers, just because.
2. Buy them something they've been wanting for a while.
3. Send them a surprise package at work.
4. Make them a mix CD and explain why you chose each song for them.
5. Sign them up for a class they've been wanting to take.

6. Tickets to a drive-in to see their favourite movie (and don't forget to pack some snacks!).
7. A candle in their favourite scent.
8. A Christmas ornament from every place you visit.
9. That book they've been talking about for weeks.
10. A pretty flower plucked from the garden and presented with fanfare.

HOW TO INCORPORATE QUALITY TIME

1. Plan regular date nights.
2. Turn off your phones when you are out together.
3. Consider a 'chore date': Turn boring errands into together time.
4. If one of you is out of town, set time aside for Skype or Zoom dates.
5. Take a cooking class together or take up any hobby together.
6. Find a list of 'trips' around where you live and become tourists in your own area.
7. Plan a picnic at the local park. Enjoy the sun and each other.
8. Take a nap together—other activities are optional. Cuddling is underrated!
9. Read the same book and discuss it together.
10. Turn doing typically boring tasks like bills or meal planning into quality time, as you together decide how you will spend your entertainment budget for the month.

Chapter 6

Third Wheeling

Triangulation in Relationships

'My mom always told me to be careful of girls who were the only child,' Ankit almost sputters out in disgust.

I look at him. This is my first session with Ankit. Ankit is a 35-year-old, struggling with a very recent separation from his wife of one-and-a-half years, Urvi. His brow is frowned, he is visibly irritated and surely his wife's height couldn't be the only reason for his condition. I urge him to elaborate.

'Urvi is nice okay, I am not complaining, but the whole point of this is to be with our parents and together.'

'And this is not what Urvi wants?' I enquire.

'No, she wants that. See, she has lived in a joint family all her life, and she likes the hustle and bustle of life and family together. She was doing pretty well, too. But it's just that it was weird. I mean, I really don't know the problem, that's why I am here, right?'

I nod briefly. He doesn't know his problem but he knows he is not okay with what he is doing and how his life looks like right now. That's a problem enough.

'I understand this might be really overwhelming for you right now, Ankit, but for me to better understand, tell me, was this separation initiated mutually?'

'Mutually, meaning? She wanted it and I wanted it? Yeah.' He stops. 'I guess. I mean, how can one live with constant bickering like that?'

'But there were discussions about what the separation would look like?'

'Of course. She wanted nothing from me, I wanted nothing from her, and that's it.'

'Hmm, so tell me, when did problems first start to crop up?'

'Okay, problems.' Ankit's phone rings in his pocket. He immediately pulls it out and looks at me. 'I am sorry, but I have to take this.'

I nod.

'Haanji, pranam Mummy, boliye, tell me. Haan main araha hu ghar, I'm coming home in half an hour. Yes... yes, we'll go then. Okay, bye.'

He puts his phone away and looks at me. 'Sorry, sorry, actually she doesn't know I am here. She will get really worried ke kuch garbar ho gaya hai, that something's up,' he says, gesturing to his brain.

I smile. 'I understand, no worries. As long as you keep it short, just like you did right now.' He laughs.

'Problems?' I prompt.

'Haan problems, hmm, Urvi didn't cook often. She hated rotis, and my family loves rotis. Urvi didn't really care about her home clothes. That was a big issue. She was always wearing like short stuff. Now, at home with everyone present, it doesn't look nice no. Yeah.'

'Go on, anything else that comes to your mind?'

'She really spoke her mind, she didn't hold back at all. At all.'

'And...?'

'And yeah, she didn't want a kid.'

'Okay, and you wanted one?'

'Yes, absolutely. I mean, kids do keep the house together, don't they? At least if we had a kid, maybe things wouldn't be as bad as they are today.'

'Okay. Of all the things you pointed out Ankit, I hear a lot of "my family hated it, my family didn't really like it". I want to know about *you*. What specific problems do you think you had with Urvi in these one and a half years of marriage and living together?'

He smiles weakly. 'My family's problems are my problems, right?'

'But surely there are some things that you solely had a problem with, that your family didn't or still don't know of?'

'Now that you are making me think, nothing specific comes to my mind. Except for the ones that I already shared.'

'Okay, so when those things were happening—when these problems were cropping up—do you remember how you felt?'

'Yeah, I remember coming home every day from the office to this weird silence; it was so heavy, the silence hurt my ear. I would immediately know that there was something wrong and something had happened. I used to feel very hurt, you know...I thought that my marriage would be a source of happiness to my family. I always envisioned a quintessential hasta-khelta parivaar, a happy-go-lucky family, but the last year and a half has really hurt me. I almost feel broken. It is sad to admit this. I don't want to feel like a failure, but I also feel so ashamed,' he pauses.

'Ashamed, that is a big one.'

'Yeah, ashamed of the fact that I couldn't manage my wife, nor my marriage. I couldn't make my parents happy. I couldn't really give them the peace that they deserve.' He looks away. 'I am sorry.'

'Ankit, please don't apologise. These are your emotions and they are all very valid, and I am proud of you for being able to express them so well.'

'Thank you,' he says softly.

'Shall we go back to how the early days of the marriage were?'

'Yeah, so we got married after a few months of dating. It was a love-cum-arranged setup. Urvi actually is a close friend of my cousin's family. So that's how we got to know each other. And I really liked her on the first go. I was looking for marriage and she was as well. So we both knew early on that it was going to be serious. And it was. Our dating phase went quite well actually. Urvi was the kind of person who spoke her mind, took decisions, had a very good job. She loved her job. And was an avid traveller.'

'So you are saying that there were many qualities that attracted you to her, including her opinionated personality and independence? Also, it helped that both of you were ready to take things in the relationship to the next level, would that be right?'

'Yes, that's right. Also, she was very social.' Ankit's

face lights up. 'She was...*is*...an extrovert, whereas I have been an introvert all my life. I guess she had all the things I didn't have, heh. But I guess, my mom was always too skeptical of this relationship. She has been very protective of me, naturally, and choosing a girl for marriage was of course a very important decision. She did ask me multiple times if I was sure or not.'

'Did she get along with Urvi?'

'Mom? In the beginning yes. In fact, during the dating phase, she tried very hard to get to know her. And interestingly, Mom and Urvi speak till date. I am the one who has no contact with her. Haha. That's funny, no?'

'Hmm, so you mentioned you felt like your mom was skeptical. Any specific concerns she had about her?'

'Yeah, no, she absolutely told me she was skeptical about Urvi's background. She also expressed concern about how she would manage job and the family. She spoke about how Urvi was a very pampered kid, being the only child and all, so how would she adjust? She also particularly asked me to have a conversation with her about her clothing preference while we were dating.'

'Did you?'

'No, it was too awkward for me.'

'Ankit, if you were to wake up tomorrow, and you had the power to change the past one and a half years, what would you change? Imagine you have the ability to turn back time and change anything and everything. What would those things be?'

Ankit sighs.

Over the next several weeks, we speak at length about the things he mentioned that he would change. But before

I tell you what those were, let me tell you how he reached those realisations. During those sessions, we discussed the impact of a possibly well-meaning third party and how it impacts a relationship.

Think about a game of tug-of-war. Ideally, there are two teams, holding onto either end of the rope, right? What would happen if there were three teams? Would that game be possible? Maybe it would be, but there would be a lot of chaos, right?

Our emotional connections can be compared to a game of tug-of-war. Instead of two teams pulling on the rope, there are three. The two people hold onto either end of the rope, representing their connection to each other. When one person pulls, it affects the tension felt by the other, creating a delicate balance. Now, imagine that instead of communicating directly with each other, these individuals start pulling in a third person. This third person becomes the pivot point, the focal point of attention, and the source of validation or conflict resolution. The dynamics shift constantly, with each person vying for support or alliance from the said third party.

Just as in a physical tug-of-war, this emotional tug-of-war becomes strained and unpredictable. The rope may fray, tensions may rise, and ultimately, the connections between the individuals become tangled and strained. What started as a simple game of pull and release becomes a complex web of emotions, alliances, and power struggles.

Makes sense?

Technically, this is what we call Triangulation. Triangulation is when any third party occupies a pivotal role in the quality of the relationship between two people.

The third party has a lot of power over how the relationship between the other two turns out. Triangulation is so common in households and workplaces that it has almost been normalised. Triangulation can be intentional or unintentional. But that being said, it often starts because the relationship between the two people does not have clear authentic communication. They are either prone to misunderstanding and conflicts or lack self-awareness and conscious behaviour. Either one goes to a seemingly trustworthy third party. This third party feels the need to be involved directly rather than sending them to solve matters on their own because they feel the need to be in control, power, and position. This stems from a certain fear or insecurity of losing the said qualities in their (the third party's) own life.

What are some instances of triangulation in a relationship?

1. In a family, a child might become the focus of attention in a parental conflict, with each parent seeking support or validation from the child, thereby creating a triangular dynamic.
2. Triangulation can occur when one partner seeks emotional support or validation from someone outside the relationship due to perceived deficiencies in the attachment bond with their partner. This can lead to feelings of insecurity and jealousy within the relationship.
3. Triangulation can also manifest in communication patterns within couples or families. For instance, rather than addressing issues directly with their partner, an individual might confide in a friend or

family member, creating a communication triangle that undermines trust and intimacy.

4. In some cases, triangulation can be a manifestation of power struggles within relationships. For example, a partner might triangulate by aligning with a third party to exert control or manipulate their partner's behaviour, leading to feelings of coercion and resentment.

In my sessions with Ankit, we also discussed how triangulation can show itself in relationships and how to recognise when outside help is truly helpful or not.

To be able to understand a triangulation scenario requires self-awareness and attentiveness to the relationship dynamics. Here are some signs that you might be in a triangulation situation:

1. **Communication Breakdown:** If you find it challenging to communicate directly with your partner or if important discussions often involve a third party, this could be a sign of triangulation. For example, you might frequently confide in friends or family members instead of addressing issues directly with your partner.
2. **Feeling Caught in the Middle:** If you feel like you're constantly being pulled between your partner and another person, such as a friend, family member, or colleague, it could indicate triangulation. You might feel pressured to take sides or act as a mediator in conflicts between them.
3. **Emotional Instability:** Triangulation can lead to emotional instability and uncertainty within the

relationship. You might experience feelings of jealousy, insecurity, or mistrust, especially if your partner seeks emotional support or validation from someone else.

4. **Shifting Alliances:** In a triangulation scenario, alliances and loyalties may shift frequently. You might notice your partner forming close bonds with other individuals or seeking validation from different sources, causing fluctuations in the dynamics of your relationship.
5. **Difficulty Resolving Conflict:** If conflicts within your relationship seem to escalate or remain unresolved despite your efforts to address them, it could be a sign of triangulation. Involving third parties in conflicts may hinder effective communication and problem-solving between you and your partner.
6. **Lack of Boundaries:** Triangulation often involves blurred boundaries between individuals, with one person intruding into the relationship dynamics of another. If you feel that your personal space or privacy is consistently violated by outside influences, it could indicate triangulation.

How do we realise when a possible well-meaning individual is actually causing more harm than good?

Family is a big part of a marriage, especially in South Asian communities. In cultures where family involvement in decision-making is prevalent, triangulation can often be a common occurrence. Family plays a central role in the lives of individuals in these communities, and decisions regarding marriage, career, and even daily life are often made collectively, with input from elders and extended family members.

One of the key factors contributing to triangulation in these cultures is the value placed on elder advice and wisdom. Elders are respected figures whose opinions are highly regarded and sought after in matters of importance, including relationships. However, despite the intention to seek guidance and support, the involvement of elders in intimate details of couples' lives can sometimes lead to unintended consequences.

One of the challenges is that elders, like all individuals, carry their own set of experiences, beliefs, and emotional wounds. Consciously or unconsciously, they may project their own unresolved issues onto the couples seeking their advice. For example, an elder who experienced marital conflict or dysfunction in their own relationship may inadvertently influence a couple's dynamics based on their own biases or unhealed wounds.

Furthermore, the intergenerational gap between elders and younger couples can lead to misunderstandings and miscommunication. Elders may hold traditional views or expectations regarding marriage and relationships that may not align with the values or lifestyles of younger generations. This disconnect can create tension and conflict within the family dynamic, further exacerbating triangulation.

A huge speedbump that couples frequently encounter is that more often than not, the involvement of elders in intimate details of the couples' lives leads to a loss of privacy and autonomy within the relationship. Couples may feel pressured to conform to familial expectations or decisions, even if they conflict with their own desires or beliefs. This can strain the couple's relationship and erode trust and intimacy over time.

Some signs to be wary of that a helpful family member is not that helpful in reality:

1. **They Often Try to Play Mediator:** A family member may position themselves as a mediator or go-between for the couple, offering unsolicited advice, opinions, or judgments about the relationship dynamics.
2. **They Take Sides:** The family member may openly take sides in conflicts between the couple, expressing favouritism towards one partner and criticising or blaming the other.
3. **Talking to Them Fuels Conflict:** They may inadvertently or intentionally exacerbate conflicts between the couple by stirring up drama, gossiping, or sharing private information without consent.
4. **Trust Is Decreasing between the Couple:** The family member's involvement in the couple's relationship can undermine trust and intimacy, leading to feelings of betrayal and resentment.
5. **They Interfere in Decision-Making:** The family member may insert themselves into the couple's decision-making process, offering unsolicited opinions or attempting to control their choices.
6. **They Have No Concept of Boundaries:** They may disregard boundaries within the couple's relationship, intruding into private matters or attempting to dictate the terms of their interactions.

7. **They Are Good at Inducing Guilt:** The family member may use guilt-tripping or manipulation tactics to influence the couple's behaviour or decisions, playing on their sense of obligation or loyalty.

So, should we never ask for help then? Are we supposed to figure out everything, know everything and just move on with life individually?

The question of when to ask for help is a nuanced one, with considerations ranging from the nature of the problem to the dynamics of personal relationships. While seeking assistance can be crucial in navigating challenges, it's essential to discern the right time and the right person to approach.

Debates often arise regarding the appropriateness of seeking help, with some advocating for independence and self-reliance, while others emphasise the importance of reaching out for support when needed. The truth lies somewhere in between. While self-sufficiency is admirable, there are times when seeking external guidance can lead to more effective problem-solving and personal growth.

Choosing the right person to act as a mediator or confidant is paramount in this process. While friends and family members may seem like natural choices, their inherent biases and personal experiences can inadvertently exacerbate the situation. Those close to us may project their own fears, insecurities, or past traumas onto our circumstances, clouding their judgment and hindering their ability to provide impartial advice.

In selecting a mediator, it's essential to prioritise objectivity and empathy. Ideally, this individual should possess a combination of emotional intelligence, communication skills, and a willingness to listen without judgment. They should be able to offer perspective and guidance without imposing their own agenda or biases onto the situation.

Effective communication is key in navigating challenges within a relationship. Couples must cultivate an open and honest dialogue, where both partners feel heard, valued, and supported. Approaching issues as a team, with a shared understanding that it's 'us against the world', can strengthen the bond between partners and foster a sense of unity in overcoming obstacles.

The decision to seek help should be based on individual circumstances, with careful consideration given to the nature of the problem and the dynamics of personal relationships. Choosing the right mediator is essential, as biased or uninformed advice can potentially do more harm than good.

So what did Ankit say he would have changed if he had the power to go back?

I would take things slow and communicate better.

'All my life, I have been the silent type. I have always listened, especially to my mother, and have strived very hard to not disappoint her. I have done everything I can to please her—right from being an engineer to pursuing that Marketing degree, when I actually wanted to be a teacher. But I couldn't even accept that dream for myself. A teacher was not the dream that was glorified in my household. My dad was pretty successful in his business but he never really encouraged me to follow his trail. He would always be away. I think Dad did a good job of evading all household responsibilities under the pretext of a hectic business schedule.

'I wonder if Mom ever felt alone. She did, I guess. So she made her three kids her life. She was the one who took me to school, my sister to her tuition, and bhai to his sports coaching. But I have to give it to my elder brother, he did manage to build his own thing. Mom wasn't pleased at all, though. She feels that he betrayed her. After everything she did for him, he didn't stay with us. He left to pursue his sports passion and didn't even look back. My mother hasn't been in frequent touch with him since. Neither have I. I think only my sister calls him. And maybe Dad, I don't know. My sister wasn't really pressurised, maybe because Mom always knew she was going to get married off and build a family of her own.

'But yeah, the only time I didn't pay much heed to her words was during this marriage thing with Urvi. I was confused, you know. She was so good to Urvi, like she spoke to her every day, and both of them went out for coffee and dinner together and stuff man. I thought she really liked her.'

'And she didn't?' I interject.

'Huh, I mean, she never attempted to stop Urvi or tell me to think differently. Didn't she want my marriage to succeed?'

'Hmm, you mentioned communicating better. Tell me more.'

'Yeah, I would communicate it to Urvi, how much this marriage meant to me. I always assumed she knew and would understand. There were times when she begged me to speak and take a stand, but I didn't. I could have, but maybe I didn't know how. I was never put in that position before. And I failed to understand that it was important for the relationship.'

I would perhaps not take my troubles to my mother.

'While my mother had/has the best of intentions for my life, I feel like somewhere she did take things very personally. The advice or perspective that she was giving me wasn't unbiased. It was from the perspective of how I need to protect myself, instead of looking at the problem as something to be solved. I started looking at the problems as something that was a dead end. I either lived with it unhappily or remained quiet. Of course, at that point, Urvi and I should have been having frequent communication.

'Mom has had her own share of troubles, I understand that. And that is why I never wanted to disappoint her. You know, Mom struggled in her marriage. In fact, Dad was rarely home as I said, but Mom was never truly able to accept this, I guess. She's never seen herself as a victim. Always in control. Never emotional. Always doing what she deemed best.

'And somewhere…' his voice breaks, '…maybe…'

'Yes. Go on.'

'Maybe Mom felt like she was losing me?' He looks at me. The guilt and shame he spoke of earlier is evident on his face.

I nod. 'You realised your Mom started to feel lonely after your marriage?'

'No, not lonely per se. She has a great circle of good friends, and of course, her work keeps her busy and involved, but Urvi, you know, is a very independent thinker. She was raised in a joint family, yes; she is also very close to her family members, but she has always done her own thing. And she has always asked me to do my own thing as well. And somehow, maybe that didn't really sit well and was noticeable to Mom, you know. I understand, because she might have felt like she was no longer needed.'

'So did you feel like now the role of her as a mother was extinct or not needed?'

'No absolutely not. In fact, I was happy that I had the right kind of decision-making capacity. I felt independent, free almost. Or so I thought.'

I would be discerning and maintain necessary boundaries.

'I realise now that I would just share a lot of our relationship details with my family in general. Just seemingly innocent details about our talks and habits or quirks or even perspectives that Urvi had shared. I now have come to realise that every bit of that was received with judgment—almost like everybody was waiting to point out what is wrong instead of just taking in the information unbiasedly or as a bonding technique to know our relationship better.

'A bit of a comment here, a snide remark there—it is apparent that my family members were not simply absorbing these details with an open mind or using them as a means to better understand our relationship. Instead, there seemed to be an underlying expectation that something would be found wanting or that flaws would be uncovered. It felt as though they were waiting to pounce on any perceived shortcomings, ready to criticise rather than offer constructive feedback or support.

'This realisation has honestly been eye-opening

for me, because I realise the importance of discretion and discernment in sharing the intimate details of our relationship. While I understand it's only natural to want to share experiences with trusted loved ones, it's also equally essential to consider the context and potential biases of those we confide in.'

I nod. 'That's a big one, Ankit. Not everyone will approach your relationship with the same level of objectivity or empathy that we hope for, and inadvertently exposing vulnerabilities to judgment can unnecessarily strain both the relationship and our familial bonds.'

I would enforce autonomy, even if it felt weird and awkward.

'I would consciously enforce my autonomy, even if it initially felt uncomfortable and awkward. Growing up, I have always been seen as the "golden child" by my mother, and perhaps she has come to expect me to always go along with her wishes without question. However, I realise that this perception wasn't necessarily an accurate reflection of my true self. I know now deep down that I need to assert myself and make decisions based on my own thoughts and desires, rather than simply conforming to others' expectations.

'It will be so challenging, though,' he laughs weakly.

'Speaking up and asserting my opinions feels unfamiliar, but I know I will have to face my feelings of guilt or fear of disappointing others.'

'Absolutely, Ankit. With time and practice, we can learn to embrace this newfound sense of autonomy and confidence in our own judgment. You can relearn to trust yourself and your instincts, and gradually, speak your mind, assert boundaries, operate from your inner compass. While it may, in fact it *will*, feel daunting at first, reclaiming your autonomy will allow you to step into your own power and live life on your own terms, unafraid to chart your own path and make decisions that align with your true self.'

I would identify my needs and define marriage and relationships for myself, not act upon someone else's definition.

'I've come to realise that many of us unconsciously replicate our parents' marriages in our own relationships, simply because that's the model we've been exposed to. Behaviours that may not serve us well or even be harmful have been normalised, while healthier alternatives may have been overlooked or disregarded.

'I want to question these ingrained patterns and reflect on my own beliefs and needs. By doing so, maybe I can be fair to my relationship? I want to take ownership of my choices and redefine what marriage and relationships mean to me.

'Do you think Urvi and I can work out?' He looks at me questioningly.

'That's a conversation you must be ready to have directly with her, don't you think?'

He nods.

His phone vibrates, puncturing the silence in the room. He looks at me. I nod a go-ahead.

He answers.

'Haanji Mumma, I am in my therapy session. Give you a call as soon as I am out, okay? Yep, bye.'

I smile and make a tiny note, 'Progress.'

If you feel it is impossible, given the family dynamics you are in, I urge you to think again. Self-autonomy doesn't have to be a huge statement. It can be something as simple as a small action you take for YOUR well-being. Self-expression is a fundamental aspect of autonomy, and it empowers individuals to assert their needs, beliefs, and desires in the world. Your voice is a powerful tool, and it's about using your voice, even when it feels uncomfortable or uncertain, because your perspective matters and deserves to be heard.

Showing self-autonomy within a family can look like setting boundaries and asserting oneself respectfully yet decisively. It means expressing your needs and preferences without fear of backlash or criticism, while also respecting the autonomy and boundaries of others.

Establishing autonomy involves open communication, active listening, and mutual respect, creating an environment where each family member feels valued and heard.

1. **Setting Boundaries:** Each family member has the right to establish personal boundaries regarding their time, space, and emotional needs. Self-autonomy in a family involves respecting these boundaries and communicating them clearly to others.
2. **Making Decisions Independently:** Encouraging family members to make decisions autonomously, whether it's about their education, career, or personal goals. Supporting each other's choices, even if they differ from one's own, fosters a sense of empowerment and mutual respect.

3. **Open Communication:** Promoting an environment where family members feel comfortable expressing their thoughts, feelings, and concerns without fear of judgment or reprisal. Active listening and validation of each other's perspectives contribute to a culture of mutual understanding and empathy.
4. **Shared Responsibilities:** Distributing household responsibilities equitably among family members and allowing individuals to contribute according to their abilities and interests. Recognising and valuing each person's unique contributions fosters a sense of autonomy and self-worth within the family unit.
5. **Respecting Differences:** Embracing diversity and honouring each family member's individuality, including their cultural, religious, or personal beliefs. Celebrating differences rather than imposing conformity encourages self-expression and autonomy within the family dynamic.

Here are some small but powerful behaviour changes that can help you:

1. **Practice Saying No:** Start saying no to requests or commitments that don't align with your priorities or values. This helps assert your boundaries and prioritise your own needs.
2. **Make Decisions Independently:** Take small decisions on your own, such as choosing what to eat for dinner or which movie to watch. Trust your instincts and preferences without seeking approval from others.

3. **Express Your Opinions:** Share your thoughts and ideas in conversations, even if they differ from the majority. Your perspective is valid, and speaking up helps assert your autonomy and contributes to meaningful discussions.
4. **Set Personal Goals:** Identify goals that are important to you, whether they're related to career, health, relationships, or personal growth. Take proactive steps towards achieving them, empowering yourself to shape your own future.
5. **Prioritise Self-Care:** Dedicate time each day to activities that nourish your physical, emotional, and mental well-being. Whether it's exercise, meditation, hobbies, or relaxation, prioritise self-care as a way of honouring your needs and nurturing your autonomy.

As babies, we instinctively cry to communicate our needs, but as we grow older, we often learn to silence ourselves. Why? Maybe we are riddled with the fear of rejection, judgment, or discomfort. Maybe we all want to be the golden child. Maybe we internalise societal norms and expectations, conforming to what is deemed acceptable or appropriate, even if it means suppressing our true thoughts and emotions.

But true autonomy requires breaking free from these constraints and reclaiming our voice. True autonomy is getting in touch with our inner selves and acting out of that alignment.

Chapter 7

Not Good Enough

How Perfectionism Can Be Sabotaging

Somya has just finished her three-hour meeting. She stretches her back while the balcony curtain dances around beautifully. Her 38th-floor apartment has the perfect views and the perfect sunlight. It took her six months to find this house. Those six months were complete chaos, obviously. It saw her operating from her friend's places, or hole-in-the-wall cafes, and for a month at her ex-boyfriend's place. And of course, living out of suitcases. But it was so worth it in the end. Somya sips some very black coffee as she checks her schedule. Today she has seven more meetings along with a date night. The calendar also had two dates marked in for tomorrow and three other dates planned meticulously on the weekend.

As she checks her calendar her phone buzzes. She has 10 new Bumble/Hinge/Tinder notifications. Somya is on all dating apps and is actively looking to get settled. Her father is after her life to see her get married and she also feels like she has the capacity to finally settle down. She mindlessly clears all of her notifications and takes a deep breath before lighting her cigarette. A seven-figure income, a great house, a great job, some great friends, a very expensive bar. What else does life need?

She opens her app to order. Twenty odd restaurants are providing buy-1 get-1 offers. She scrolls through all of them and then exasperatedly puts her phone down. There are SO many options.

She goes to her fridge. There are some 10 bottles of sparkling water. She grabs one and puts it away only to grab a protein bar and go to her balcony. She still has seven and a half minutes before her next meeting. She might as well decide what to wear for her date tonight.

It is not that she hasn't met men she likes. But weirdly, in these 37 years of existence, she has yet to find one that aligns with her completely. It is worth fighting for your love story, no? She has met very nice men in fact. But things haven't progressed to marriage.

There were two times that it did, and one even went to an engagement. But that's when things fell through. So many loopholes, so many doubts, and so many fears came through that she called it off. Somya believes that when something is meant for her it will come to her.

But she also realises that she has to put herself out there, so she is trying. It isn't easy but she has a plan—work and go for dates. That's her strategy. In fact, in her mind it is the perfect strategy. This *has* to work. As you meet more people, she thinks, the probability increases of finding the one who completely understands and aligns with her. She thinks as she scans her closet for an outfit. She is determined to find her perfect partner. She knows she deserves someone amazing.

A piece of ribbon sticks out oddly amidst the immaculately folded clothing. She frowns as she tucks it in place. She is going to be a great partner. She has always been the better partner anyway.

It is Sunday evening. As Monday looms on the horizon, Somya lays on the couch, scrolling through Instagram. She curses herself for not resting properly that weekend while liking photos of her friends on vacations with spouses and husbands. There was this one—a year junior, very average student—now somewhere in a valley, chilling in a 100-acre farmhouse she owns. She scrolls past another friend of hers, Mugdha, who has turned into a couple vlogger after her marriage—what a romantic life! Every day was a date night or something as exciting. How were women finding these men?

A message pops up. It is from the guy she went out with yesterday. She rolls her eyes as she dismisses the notification. She wasn't particularly impressed. In fact, all the dates she has been on have been good. Yep, just that. Good. Nothing great. Nothing amazing.

One man was cute, she wouldn't lie. But would he be a good partner? She didn't get that vibe from him. Maybe they could go out again.

As the TV softly plays her favourite series in the background, she turns to her phone to swipe for more 'great' men that she knows are out there. She is hopeful, of course. Which app should she open, though? The last two dates were from Hinge. Should she open Bumble or did Tinder have better men? She decides to read an article on it first. Maybe the internet has some statistics on which app has a higher success rate?

She is determined to find the perfect platform, the perfect man, and build her perfect happily ever after with him. Nothing can stop her from living her dream.

Somya's experience is not unique; she is part of a larger societal trend. In today's fast-paced world, characterised by technological advancements and a plethora of choices in every aspect of life, many of us find ourselves caught up in a whirlwind of mindlessness and overconsumption. From clothing and food to the endless stream of digital content, we are bombarded with options at every turn, fostering a culture of instant gratification and a relentless pursuit of excellence, of the best, of the perfect option for us.

We often find ourselves trapped in a cycle of comparison and competition, driven by a singular focus on productivity, achievement, and success. We are constantly striving to outperform others and win a race whose endpoint remains elusive and undefined.

What's particularly ironic is that despite the absence of external barriers, many individuals like Somya find themselves stuck in a state of limbo, unable to move forward. The primary obstacle they face is not external circumstances or the actions of others, but rather their own internalised notions of perfectionism and high standards.

These self-imposed standards create a constant sense of pressure and dissatisfaction, as individuals relentlessly pursue an unattainable ideal of perfection. They become their own harshest critics, constantly striving for excellence while simultaneously feeling inadequate and unfulfilled.

In this quest for perfection, individuals often overlook the toll it takes on their mental and emotional well-being. The relentless pressure to excel leads to burnout, anxiety, and a pervasive sense of inadequacy. Despite the abundance of choices and opportunities available, many perfectionists find themselves paralysed by fear of failure or unable to make decisions for fear of making the wrong choice.

Moreover, perfectionism fosters a narrow focus on productivity and external validation, detracting from the richness and depth of human experience. Instead of savouring the journey and embracing life's imperfections, perfectionists fixate on outcomes and achievements, measuring their self-worth by external standards rather than internal fulfilment.

I would like to tell you that being a perfectionist is not a compliment. Well, not wholly. You see, perfectionism exists on a spectrum. Being a perfectionist usually refers to qualities in an individual like a high standard, exceptional performance, and resilience.

However, the reality is more nuanced. While it can indeed drive individuals to achieve greatness, it also comes with significant drawbacks.

At one end of the spectrum, perfectionism can lead to higher standards and better performance. Individuals with perfectionistic tendencies often strive for excellence in their endeavours, pushing themselves to go above and beyond to achieve their goals. They may possess a strong work ethic, attention to detail, and a drive for continuous improvement, all of which can contribute to success in various aspects of life. However, on the other end of the spectrum, perfectionism more often than not results in unrealistic expectations and a relentless pursuit of flawlessness. This relentless pursuit can lead to a variety of negative consequences, including burnout, loss of balance, and impaired well-being.

Perfectionists may find themselves trapped in a cycle of striving for unattainable ideals, constantly feeling like they fall short of their own impossibly high standards. This can lead to chronic stress, anxiety, and dissatisfaction, as they struggle to meet the unrealistic demands they place on themselves.

An underexplored part of perfectionism is that it can also take a toll on relationships and personal well-being. The constant pressure to be perfect can lead to feelings of inadequacy and self-doubt, as individuals may fear failure or judgment from others. This can result in social isolation, difficulty forming meaningful connections, and an overall unseen struggle with themselves and the outer world. Perfectionistic tendencies have significantly increased among young people over the past 30 years (Curran, T., & Hill, A. (2017). 'Perfectionism Is Increasing Over Time: A meta-analysis of birth cohort differences from 1989 to 2016'. *Psychological Bulletin*, University of Bath and York St. John University), regardless of gender or culture. Factors such as greater academic and professional competition, along with the pervasive influence of social media and its tendency to encourage harmful comparisons, are believed to contribute to this rise.

Did you know that perfectionism can be categorised into different kinds? It is a complex and layered trait after all.

1. **Self-Oriented Perfectionism:** This type of perfectionism involves setting excessively high standards for oneself and striving for flawlessness in personal endeavours. In the academic or professional sphere, individuals with self-oriented

perfectionism may obsessively pursue excellence, seeking to achieve top grades or attain career success at all costs.

2. **Other-Oriented Perfectionism:** This form of perfectionism revolves around holding others to unrealistic standards and expecting perfection from them. In interpersonal relationships, individuals with other-oriented perfectionism may impose their expectations on partners, family members, or colleagues, leading to strained relationships and conflict.
3. **Socially Prescribed Perfectionism:** Socially prescribed perfectionism involves internalising societal or cultural expectations of perfection and feeling immense pressure to meet these standards. In the realm of social media, individuals may compare themselves to idealised images and lifestyles portrayed online, leading to feelings of inadequacy and low self-esteem.

Perfectionism can also be either overt or covert, that is, an individual may openly and proudly accept that they are perfectionists and live life that way. But covert perfectionists are actually subtle people and they do not make their perfectionism known because they sometimes do not acknowledge it themselves but internalise it and struggle with rigidity and high standards alone.

Recognising the traits of perfectionism and determining if they are dysfunctional can be challenging but crucial for personal growth and well-being. Here are some signs that perfectionism may be detrimental:

1. **Rigid Standards:** Setting excessively high standards for oneself that are unattainable or unrealistic. Imagine someone who sets impossibly high standards for themselves at work. They expect nothing less than perfection in every project they tackle, often staying late at the office to ensure every detail is flawless. Despite receiving praise from their colleagues, this person constantly feels stressed and overwhelmed, as they can never quite meet their own sky-high expectations.
2. **All-or-Nothing Thinking:** A sure-shot way to feel defeated is through this cognitive distortion—viewing success and failure in black-and-white terms, with little room for nuance or flexibility. Imagine someone who, when they don't ace a presentation at work, consider it a total failure, overlooking the valuable feedback they received from their team. This all-or-nothing mindset leaves them feeling defeated and demoralised, even when they are making progress.
3. **Procrastination:** Avoiding tasks or projects for fear of not being able to meet one's own standards of perfection. You definitely know someone who has BIG goals but constantly puts off starting that new project. Most likely it is because they fear they won't be able to meet their own standards of perfection. Instead of diving in and getting started, they find themselves endlessly researching or organising their workspace, delaying the inevitable and increasing their stress levels in the process. In fact, people with perfectionism can suffer from

Perfection Paralysis. It looks a little like: Can I be the perfect partner? I don't know, I'd rather not falter so I will not even get to know them. Or, what if my business idea fails? I will wait for the perfect time—when I am ready to start, when the world is more accepting etc.

4. **Self-Criticism:** Most perfectionists struggle with this. Engaging in harsh self-criticism or self-blame when expectations are not met. They themselves are their own harshest critic. When they fall short of their own expectations, they berate themselves with negative self-talk, convinced that they're not good enough. This constant self-criticism takes a toll on their confidence and self-esteem, making it even harder for them to bounce back from setbacks.
5. **Impaired Relationships:** A lesser known and talked about aspect of perfectionism is that perfectionists often struggle deeply in relationships due to their tendency to build walls and resist vulnerability. They may have rigid perspectives of what an ideal relationship should look like, based on unrealistic standards and expectations. This rigid mindset can prevent them from fully opening up to their partner and embracing the messy, imperfect aspects of a human connection.

Perfectionists may also find it challenging to let their guard down and be vulnerable with their partner, fearing judgment or rejection if they reveal their true selves. They may prioritise maintaining a facade of perfection, presenting only the polished and curated version of themselves to the outside world. This reluctance to show vulnerability can create a barrier to intimacy and hinder genuine emotional connection in the relationship.

Moreover, perfectionists may struggle with relinquishing control and allowing their partner to have autonomy and agency within the relationship. They may have difficulty accepting differences of opinion or compromise, clinging to their own rigid expectations and standards. This can lead to power struggles and conflicts within the relationship, as both partners may feel stifled or unheard.

So what do we do? Do we just let go of our standards? Do we just settle for what comes our way? Do we just let go of our needs and expectations?

Absolutely not. I am not suggesting that because you are a perfectionist you will now have to not be one *at all*. Remember how we spoke of perfectionism existing on a spectrum? Try to think of your expectations in the grays. It is about finding the sweet spot that works for you. Or as psychoanalyst Donald Winnicott put it, try thinking about it from a POV of 'good enough'.

Dr Winnicott introduced the concept of 'good enough'. It is, I believe, a crucial part of building healthy relationships, whether you identify as a perfectionist or not.

But first, what does the 'good enough' perspective suggest? Dr Winnicott proposed this theory in context of the mother-child relationship in his work on object relations theory (Winnicott, D. 1960. 'The Theory of the Parent-Infant Relationship'. *International Journal of Psycho-Analysis*. 411. pp.585-595).

According to Winnicott, a 'good enough' mother is not necessarily a perfect mother—a mother without any flaws or a mother who never fails or makes the wrong decisions—but rather a mother who is attuned to her infant's needs and is able to provide consistent care and support. This concept extends beyond parenting to various aspects of life, including relationships.

In the context of relationships and perfectionism, the concept of 'good enough' can be particularly relevant. Perfectionists may struggle with finding a partner who meets their idealised standards, constantly searching for someone who embodies perfection in every aspect. However, Winnicott's concept suggests that such perfection is unrealistic and unattainable.

Instead, what is needed is a partner who is *good enough*—someone who may not be flawless but is capable of providing love, support, and understanding.

From this perspective, individuals with perfectionistic tendencies may benefit from reframing their expectations and embracing the idea of a 'good enough' partner. This involves recognising that *no one is perfect* and that relationships are built on mutual acceptance, compromise, and growth. By letting go of the quest for perfection and embracing the concept of 'good enough' we can cultivate healthier and more fulfilling relationships based on realistic expectations and genuine connection.

Here is what a 'good enough' partner looks like:

1. *<u>They are attuned</u>:* A good enough partner is attuned to your emotional needs and responds with empathy and care. They listen actively, validate your feelings, and offer support without judgment.
2. *<u>They are consistent</u>*: They demonstrate reliability and

consistency in their actions and words, fostering a sense of security and trust in the relationship. You can rely on them to be there for you through both the ups and the downs.

3. *They are accepting*: They accept you for who you are, flaws and all, and celebrate your strengths and imperfections alike. They embrace your uniqueness and support your personal growth and self-discovery.
4. *They are communicative*: A good enough partner communicates openly and honestly, expressing their thoughts, feelings, and needs with respect and kindness. They encourage open dialogue and work together to resolve conflicts constructively.
5. *They are aware of boundaries*: They respect your boundaries and encourage you to establish and maintain healthy boundaries in the relationship. They understand the importance of individual autonomy and support your autonomy and independence.
6. *They are supportive of growth*: They encourage and support your personal and professional growth, cheering you on as you pursue your goals and dreams. They are your biggest cheerleader, offering encouragement and motivation along the way.
7. *They are adaptable*: They are willing to adapt and grow with you as the relationship evolves, recognising that change is a natural part of life. They approach challenges and transitions with flexibility and a willingness to learn and grow together.

8. *<u>They show genuine love</u>*: Above all, a 'good enough' partner loves you, accepts you for who you are, and stands by your side even when things are tough. Their love is not contingent on perfection but on the genuine connection and the bond you share.

What a 'good enough' partner is NOT:

1. *<u>They are NOT ABUSIVE</u>*: A good enough partner does not engage in any form of abuse, whether it's physical, emotional, or psychological. They prioritise your well-being and safety, fostering an environment of trust and safety in the relationship.
2. *<u>They do NOT give MIXED SIGNALS</u>*: A good enough partner communicates openly and honestly, and their actions match their words. They are consistent and transparent in their intentions, making it clear where they stand in the relationship.
3. *<u>They are NOT FLAKEY or DISHONEST</u>*: A good enough partner is reliable and trustworthy, honouring their commitments and staying true to their word. They do not engage in deceitful behaviour or betray your trust by cheating or being unfaithful.
4. *<u>They are NOT DISRESPECTFUL</u>*: A good enough partner treats you with kindness, empathy, and consideration, valuing your thoughts, feelings, and opinions. They do not belittle or disrespect you, nor do they undermine your self-worth or confidence. Instead, they uplift and support you, helping you to grow and thrive in the relationship.

In order for any relationship to thrive, especially those we actively choose for ourselves, it is essential to recognise that *relationships are a two-way street*. They require mutual respect, understanding, and a willingness to both give and receive love. Perfectionists may need to learn to let go of their need for control and perfection, and instead embrace the ebb and flow of partnership. Sometimes, it's about allowing themselves and their partner to flow, adapting to the ever-changing dynamics of a healthy and fulfilling relationship.

When individuals are fixated on making a perfect decision, there are so many things to consider. What will this decision look like in 10 years? What does this lead to? How will this help me in the next five years? If I am choosing my life partner, are they going to be a great parent? Is it going to be nice when we are 70?

How do we know? We are in imaginary scenarios—we haven't seen the profits being made yet on the stocks we have invested in, we haven't seen our partner as a mother or a father yet, and we aren't 70 (if any one of you is, then yes, now you know!). There are so many parameters of the future that we have no control over. Here comes something that we really need to know, and if you think it is helpful, implement it in your lives.

Instead of trying to make the perfect decision and get into a limbo—unable to experience the present and gain experience in the process—understand the concept of **satisficing**.

The words 'satisfy' and 'suffice' were combined by Herbert Simon (Simon, Herbert. 1947. *Administrative Behavior: A Study of Decision-Making Processes in*

Administrative Organization), eventually leading to the term 'satisfice'—a term used to propose an *adequate* solution rather than one that maximises utility. Opting for a 'satisficing' approach may be the optimal choice when considering the costs associated with seeking alternatives. According to Simon, because humans have limited knowledge, it's wise to take a practical approach to finding the best solutions. These solutions might not achieve the maximum possible benefits, but they are more realistic and achievable.

Isn't this a relevant approach in romantic relationships, where additional complexities arise due to our inability to predict our partner's long-term attitudes and our responses to them?

Many of us settle for the bare-minimum, so maybe there is a lot of fear and negativity around settling for something that is *just* good enough. But knowing your good enough is actually knowing yourself and your priorities, so it might not be a bad thing after all.

It's natural to strive for excellence and pursue the best possible outcomes in life. However, it's essential to recognise that settling for the 'good enough' doesn't necessarily equate to mediocrity or complacency.

Understanding what is 'good enough' for you is actually a profound act of self-awareness and prioritisation. It involves introspection and reflection on one's values, goals, and desires. By discerning what truly matters to us and aligning our choices with those priorities, we gain clarity and confidence in our decisions.

Settling for 'good enough' doesn't mean lowering our standards or compromising our ambitions. Instead, it signifies making intentional choices that honour our authentic selves and contribute to our overall well-being. It's about finding a balance between striving for improvement and accepting ourselves and our circumstances as they are.

I can help you understand that relationships, like all valuable aspects of life, require time, space, and effort to flourish and evolve. Even if you believe you have found the perfect partner, the journey doesn't end there. In fact, it's just the beginning of a shared adventure filled with growth, challenges, and shared experiences.

Even if you find the perfect partner, remember it is just the starting point, not the destination. While compatibility and alignment of values are crucial foundations, they alone are not sufficient to sustain a relationship in the long term. Both partners must actively nurture and invest in the relationship to keep it vibrant and fulfilling.

Effective communication, mutual respect, and empathy are essential ingredients for nurturing a strong and resilient bond. It's about showing up for each other, even during the challenging times, and being willing to work through conflicts and differences together. The best kind of relationships will also require ongoing adaptation and growth as individuals and as a couple. As life circumstances change and evolve, so too must the dynamics of the relationship. This may involve reevaluating priorities, setting new goals, and navigating unforeseen challenges with resilience and flexibility.

It's important to recognise that perfection is not a static state but rather a continuous journey of growth and development.

There are some areas I do see even the best of couples

ready for some battles in, and this, in turn, leads to their growth. I would like to highlight them:

1. **Communication Styles:** You and your good enough partner may have different communication styles or preferences. How both of you can communicate effectively can involve finding common ground, such as setting aside time for open and honest conversations, actively listening to each other's perspectives, and respecting each other's need for space or reflection before discussing important matters.
2. **Personal Boundaries:** Each individual has their own boundaries and comfort levels when it comes to personal space, privacy, and autonomy. Understanding personal boundaries may involve openly discussing and respecting each other's limits, negotiating compromises where necessary, and finding ways to balance individual needs with the needs of the relationship.
3. **Social Activities:** You and your good enough partner may have different preferences when it comes to socialising or spending time with friends and family. Compromising on social activities may involve finding a middle ground that respects both partners' desires, such as alternating between spending time with each other's social circles, planning activities that you both enjoy, or carving out alone time when needed.
4. **Financial Decisions:** Money can be a sensitive topic in relationships, and each partner may have

different attitudes or priorities when it comes to finances. Making smoother and better financial decisions may involve creating a budget together, discussing long-term financial goals, and finding mutually agreeable ways to manage expenses, save, and invest for the future.

5. **Household Responsibilities:** Dividing household chores and responsibilities can sometimes be a source of tension in relationships. Discussing each partner's strengths and preferences, delegating tasks fairly, and being flexible and supportive in sharing the workload based on individual schedules and commitments can help smooth functioning of the house.
6. **Career and Life Goals:** You and your partner may have different career aspirations or life goals that require understanding and support from both parties. There might be work needed in fruitfully discussing your individual priorities, finding ways to support each other's ambitions, and making joint decisions that align with your shared values and vision for the future.

This underscores the significance of understanding your priorities and needs thoroughly enough to accurately discern who a good enough partner is for you. Individuals who lack self-awareness or have weak boundaries—perhaps on account of operating under fear or societal pressure—may overlook their essential requirements in a partner.

For instance, someone who is financially stable may need a partner who shares similar financial values and stability, but they might overlook this crucial aspect and enter a relationship with someone who is just starting out financially. Similarly, an introverted individual may choose an extremely extroverted partner, leading to feelings of exhaustion and being overwhelmed by frequent social interactions.

It's crucial to recognise that a good enough partner is not necessarily the polar opposite of oneself. This decision should not be driven solely by attachment or societal norms. Instead, a good enough partner is one who meets the fundamental criteria and aligns with your core values and needs.

You must prioritise compatibility and mutual fulfillment over perfection. It involves acknowledging that no relationship is flawless and that compromises and adjustments are inevitable.

A 'good-enough partner' is a 'satisficing' partner.

Two effective ways to work on the perfectionism that stands in the way of actually living and experiencing life are working on *self-compassion* and *reducing the nagging inner voice* that is our harshest critic.

Perfectionist individuals often have high standards. These standards aren't always bad—they help us with achievement and performance. But the problem might arise when they keep raising their standards. Many perfectionists quickly disregard their achievements, unable to savour any kind of win as an achievement, and vow to do even better next time.

By continually raising their standards, these remain constantly out of reach. They then end up feeling like they are failing all the time, despite achieving outstanding results.

Another pattern that is detrimental to progress is approaching the set standards in a rigid, inflexible way. When doing well at work becomes 'I must get recognition for every project, for every presentation I make', this becomes a standard, a rule. It causes immense stress, once again leaving individuals feeling like they are failing.

Both these situations can lead to chronic self-criticism, where we just never feel like we are good enough.

Take Somya's example to help you understand what possibly could be an empowering scenario that could take her out of her perfection paralysis and help her give someone she likes a chance.

Somya is a perfectionist who is actively looking for a partner. She has high standards for herself and others, and she constantly worries about making the 'perfect' choice when it comes to dating. She meticulously analyses every potential partner, searching for flaws and imperfections. As a result, she finds herself constantly dissatisfied with her dating experiences, feeling like no one measures up to her idealised image of the perfect partner. She fears making the wrong choice and ending up in a relationship that doesn't meet her exacting standards, so she hesitates to commit to anyone.

Somya can reframe her thoughts slowly and steadily to come out of perfection paralysis. Here is how:

1. Instead of fixating on finding the perfect partner, she can shift her focus to finding someone who aligns with her core values and treats her with respect and kindness. She can remind herself that no one is perfect, and imperfections can add depth and richness to a relationship.

2. Rather than viewing dating as a quest for perfection, Somya can approach it as an opportunity for growth and self-discovery. She can embrace the journey of getting to know different people and learning more about herself in the process.
3. Somya can challenge the belief that making the 'wrong' choice in dating will lead to disaster. She can remind herself that dating is a learning experience, and each relationship, whether it lasts or not, offers valuable lessons and insights that contribute to her personal growth.
4. Instead of dwelling on her fears of rejection or failure, Somya can practice self-compassion and remind herself that it's okay to make mistakes and experience setbacks in the dating process. She can give herself permission to be imperfect and trust that she has the resilience to navigate whatever challenges come her way.

A big reason we find ourselves in this loop is also because of the inner voice that is harsh and super critical. A brilliant way to change our reality is to first be aware of our inner voice and notice what it is saying to us. The inner voice, also known as self-talk or internal dialogue, refers to the ongoing stream of thoughts and beliefs that we experience within our minds. It's the voice that narrates our experiences, interprets our emotions, and influences our perceptions of ourselves and the world around us. Becoming aware of our inner voice involves cultivating mindfulness and paying attention to the thoughts and beliefs that arise within our minds.

I find it particularly helpful to name my inner critic. By coming up with a name for my inner critic, I create a distance that allows me to not make it my identity and subconsciously create power within to change it.

My inner cititic's name is Komolika and she likes to talk a lot about me not being good enough for a lot of things. She is quite a talker, but I tell her differently. That was not the case always, though.

Let's see what Somya's inner critic might say.

1. 'You'll never find someone who meets all your standards. You're being too picky.'
2. 'You're wasting your time with this person. They're not perfect enough for you.'
3. 'If you settle for less than perfect, you'll end up unhappy and regretting your choice.'
4. 'You're not good enough for anyone to want to be with you. No one will ever measure up.'
5. 'You're making a mistake by even considering this relationship. It's not perfect, so it's not worth it.'

Reframing her inner voice to empower her instead of limiting can sound like:

1. 'You have high standards because you value yourself and what you want in a partner. It's okay to be selective.'
2. 'You're giving this person a chance to show who they are beyond your initial judgments. You're open to discovering their strengths and potential.'
3. 'Perfection doesn't exist, and that's okay. You're willing to accept imperfections and work through challenges together.'

4. 'You're worthy of love and respect, just as you are. You don't need to be perfect to be deserving of a fulfilling relationship.'
5. 'You're taking a chance on love, knowing that it comes with risks and uncertainties. You're brave for opening your heart and giving this relationship a chance to grow.'

Mugdha sits on her tiny sofa, scrolling Instagram mindlessly, dreading the Monday that looms on the horizon. She heart reacts on a picture of her college friend and an inspiring person she really looks up to, Somya. She has posted a few minutes ago. The picture is of her beautiful new flat—the views and windows are to die for. Wow, she truly has it all. Mugdha sighs in defeat as she leans back on her husband's shoulder, and continues to scroll.

Chapter 8

The Anxious-Avoidant Dance

Why Opposites First Attract and then Repel

'Why the fuck is he not replying?' Meghna looks at her roommate, exasperated, almost teary-eyed.

Oyendrila looks at her. 'Chill dude, chill. Relax and let him take some space. He will text you when he can. You don't need to get so anxious. You guys just spoke five minutes ago!'

'Yeah, I know, but I texted him after that and now he is not replying. He doesn't understand that this is important to me.'

'Ooof, I understand it is important for you. But he might also be stuck no, he might be at his parents right now, he might be driving, or something else. Maybe he is not in the headspace to respond to you at the moment.'

'No, he is chilling right now. I just know it.'

'Then maybe let him chill? Listen, I am going out to grab a coffee, do you want to come?'

'No,' Meghna says grumpily.

As Oyen heads out, Meghna feels a terrible kind of

rage. The kind of rage that clutches at your stomach, has your throat in a chokehold, and tries to burst out of your ears and eyes. She bursts into big, body-wracking sobs.

Here is she, away from home, alone and sad, while Oyen goes out for coffee freely and happily. Her partner is such a delight. She is such a confident woman. She has no dramas, no crying spells. She has it all together. Meghna howls as she drowns herself in self-pity. She left her home and found a job in Bangalore only so that she could be closer to her boyfriend, Karthik, who lives there. And now she can't even go a day without crying, without fights, and without feeling so alone. She buries her head into the pillow as she howls.

It is evening now, and Meghna is awakened by the eerie silence that evenings bring. She grabs her phone to check if Karthik has reached out. Her phone has no notifications. As she switches on the lights of the apartment, she catches her face in the mirror.

This is NOT her. She is not going to sit here crying for a man who doesn't care. She deserves better. She ties her hair into a ponytail and calls her colleague, Armeen.

'Hi babe, what's up?'

'Babe, let's go and chill somewhere?'

'Okay, do you want to hit this new cafe that has some amazing cold brew?'

'No, let's do drinks. It's Saturday night!'

'Haha okay, let's do Ole Man today? They have some offer going on, I think. I'll meet you there by 9?'

'Cool, done, see you!'

Meghna smiles, she opens Karthik's contact, hits a button and proceeds to block him on all platforms. As she is getting ready Oyen comes back.

'Hey, are you going somewhere? Did you speak to Karthik?'

'Yep, I am going to Ole Man, wanna join? It's me and Armeen. And no, no Karthik talk for tonight, please.'

Oyen lights up. 'Okay, yep, sure. Thanks, that would be fun!'

'C'mon, get ready then, we will have to reach by 9.'

Ole Man is the perfect hangout—cheap booze, near the metro station, and a fairly young crowd. As the girls pick out a table and start chatting, Meghna scans her surroundings. The crowd looks nice but why is everybody with someone? Is everyone in a relationship or what? Her eyes stop at a table adjacent to theirs where two men are smoking and chatting to each other. Heh, not bad.

One of them turns around exactly at that moment and their eyes meet. Meghna's heart misses a beat. How can a millisecond of eye contact be that electrifying? She suppresses a smile and faces her girls.

Armeen looks at her. 'What?' she asks.

Meghna signals towards the direction of those men. 'Don't look,' she mouths. They both look, of course, and laugh.

'He is looking,' Oyen says excitedly.

Meghna looks and, sure enough, he is looking in her direction. He nods at her. She smiles back, and mouths a questioning 'what' to her friends.

The night escalates pretty quickly. Within a couple of hours, all the girls and the boys are headed to an after-party. It's one in the night. As they are about to reach the party place, Oyen looks at Meghna, eyes a little wider than usual.

'What?'

'Why is Karthik calling me?' Oyen asks, holding her phone up to her friend. 'Because I blocked him, I guess,' Meghna says nonchalantly.

'What? Why did you block him? What do I say? What is this? Does he know? I don't want to be responsible. I am not responsible for anything that goes down, Meghna.'

Meghna dismisses her. 'Here give me your phone, chill.' She disconnects the call. 'See? You won't be responsible now.'

Karthik and Meghna sit in a quaint cafe for Sunday brunch. The air is tense. Karthik is quiet, unusually quiet.

'Are you okay?' Meghna asks for the fifth time. 'Yes, Meghna, stop asking me that again and again.'

'No, I feel something is truly wrong. Are you angry?'

'No, I am not.'

'No, tell me, please, I know you are angry. Is it because of last night?'

Karthik says nothing. He simply looks away.

'Fine, don't tell me. Then what is the point of sitting here? I am leaving, okay?' Meghna stands up but she doesn't move further. 'Are you going to tell me what is wrong?'

Karthik remains silent.

Meghna can't control it any longer. 'What the hell is wrong with you, man? Can't you fucking speak?' she almost shouts.

Karthik looks around. 'Don't make a scene Meghna, please. There are people here.'

'So, what? How does it matter? Do you even fucking care about me? I am here, asking you what is wrong. I haven't even slept for five hours properly. And this is the kind of treatment I get? I don't fucking deserve this. I don't.' She looks at Karthik, wanting to leave, but her feet remain glued to the ground.

Karthik looks at her and finally says, 'Okay, yeah if that's what you want.'

Meghna can't believe Karthik said that. The cab ride home is difficult. Meghna cries so much that the cabbie offers her water. That makes her cry even more. She can't help but feel like she overreacted, though. Maybe Karthik would have spoken if she had calmed down. Maybe he was just upset because she had blocked him. She can't take it anymore. She better text him before it's too late.

Through her tears, she types out a message. 'I love you, I am sorry.' Karthik immediately hearts it and responds with a GIF that says 'Me too.' Meghna sighs. She feels lighter. She feels loved. She feels okay now. She smiles a little.

What do you think? Do you think of this as romantic? As normal? As a part and parcel of a relationship?

If yes, let me tell you something—you have experienced the deep, intense pangs of attachment. And that requires a lot of understanding, awareness, and exploration to turn into a relationship that is safe and secure, has space for feelings, emotions, and perspectives of BOTH partners, and operates from a point of view of freedom rather than want, need, desire, and a constant push and pull.

After our relationship with our parents, our partnership with a romantic partner often becomes the most significant relationship in our lives. As a result, we may subconsciously view love through the lens of our experiences with our parents and behave in ways that mirror how we believe we should be loved. This can manifest in various ways, from comparing our partners to our parents to expecting them to intuitively understand our needs without us having to communicate them explicitly, akin to the way parents often anticipate and fulfil a child's needs.

It's essential to recognise that this pattern of behaviour, while understandable, does not necessarily reflect adult love. Love in adult relationships should ideally be characterised by mutual respect, open communication, and emotional reciprocity, rather than relying on implicit expectations and assumptions.

A game changer when it comes to understanding this is to familiarise ourselves with the work of psychologist John Bowlby, who studied attachment between a child and its primary caregiver, and Mary Ainsworth, who later built upon this (Bretherton, Inge. 1992. 'The Origins of Attachment Theory: John Bowlby and Mary Ainsworth'. *Developmental Psychology*. 28. pp. 759-775).

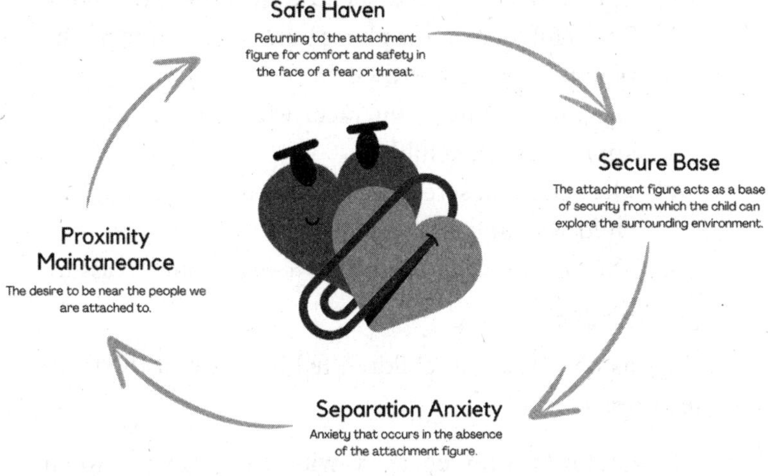

The attachment cycle

Bowlby observed that attachment was characterised by clear behavioral and motivational patterns. When children were frightened, they sought the proximity of their primary caregiver in order to receive both comfort and care.

The central theme of attachment theory is that primary caregivers who are available and responsive to an infant's needs allow the child to develop a sense of security. The infant learns that the caregiver is dependable, which creates a secure base for the child to then explore the world.

Psychologist Mary Ainsworth, in the 1970s, expanded greatly upon Bowlby's original work. In her study called 'Strange Situation', researchers observed children between the ages of 12 and 18 months as they responded to a situation in which they were briefly left alone and then reunited with their mothers.

Ainsworth's Strange Situation Assessment involved the following steps:

1. The parent and child spend time alone in a room.
2. The child freely explores the room under the parent's watchful eye.
3. A stranger enters, interacts with the parent, and approaches the child.
4. The parent discreetly exits the room, leaving the child with the stranger.
5. The parent later returns to console and reassure the child.

It was observed that children fell into one of the three categories:

1. Children who engaged with the stranger when their caregiver was present and became visibly

upset when their caregiver departed, but were happy to see the caregiver on their return. This group of children felt confident that their caregiver was available and would be responsive to their attachment needs and communications.

2. Children who avoided or ignored the caregiver, showing little emotion when the caregiver departed or returned. This group of children did not explore their environment very much regardless of who was there.
3. Children who showed signs of distress even before separation and were clingy and difficult to comfort on the caregiver's return. They showed either signs of resentment in response to the absence or signs of helpless passivity.

After analysing the participants' responses, Ainsworth identified three primary attachment styles: **secure attachment, anxious attachment,** and **avoidant attachment**.

Subsequently, researchers Main and Solomon (Main M., & Solomon J. 1986. 'Discovery of a new, insecure-disorganized/disoriented attachment pattern' in Yogman M. & Brazelton T. (Eds.), *Affective Development in Infancy*. pp. 95–124.) introduced a fourth attachment style known as **disorganised attachment**, building upon their investigations.

Attachment theory points out that our early experiences with caregivers shape our attachment styles, which in turn influence the way we form and maintain relationships throughout our lives.

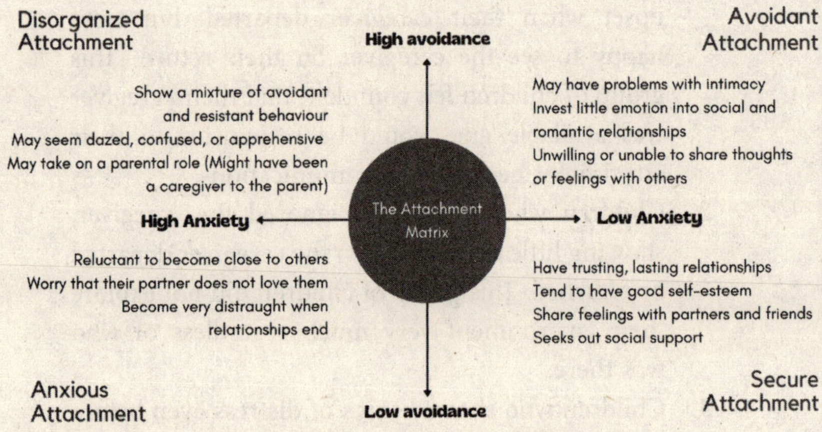

The different attachment styles

By applying the principles of attachment theory to our adult bonds, we can gain a deeper understanding of our own attachment style and how it impacts our relationships. This awareness allows us to recognise and address any unhealthy attachment patterns or behaviours that may be influencing our interactions with our partners.

Let's understand how each attachment style might look like in a romantic relationship:

Secure Attachers:

1. Express their emotions openly and honestly, fostering emotional intimacy.
2. Respect their partner's boundaries while also maintaining their own.
3. Offer support and reassurance to their partner during times of distress or uncertainty.
4. Feel comfortable with both intimacy and independence in the relationship.

5. Communicate effectively, resolving conflicts constructively and respectfully.

Anxious Attachers:

1. Seek frequent reassurance from their partner to alleviate the fear of abandonment.
2. Become anxious or distressed when their partner is unavailable or unresponsive.
3. Tend to hyperfocus on the relationship, sometimes neglecting their own needs.
4. Fear rejection and may engage in behaviours to elicit attention or closeness.
5. Have difficulty trusting their partner's intentions and may interpret ambiguous situations negatively.

Avoidant Attachers:

1. Prioritise independence and personal space, sometimes withdrawing emotionally from their partner.
2. Struggle with intimacy and vulnerability, finding it challenging to express their emotions openly.
3. Maintain emotional distance to protect themselves from potential rejection or hurt.
4. Have difficulty relying on their partner for support or comfort during times of need.
5. May avoid commitment or long-term relationships, fearing loss of autonomy or being engulfed by the relationship.

Disorganised Attachers:

1. Exhibit erratic or unpredictable behaviour in relationships, alternating between seeking closeness and withdrawing.
2. Struggle with unresolved trauma or unresolved issues from past relationships.
3. Display a lack of consistency in their responses to relational cues, leading to confusion for their partners.
4. Have difficulty regulating their emotions, resulting in volatile or chaotic interactions.
5. Experience internal conflict and ambivalence about intimacy, often oscillating between a desire for connection and a fear of being hurt or rejected.

Now that we have a basic understanding of attachment theory and its implications for romantic relationships, let's delve into a common yet highly misunderstood (or should I say, rarely understood) dynamic that many individuals encounter—anxious attachers forming relationships with avoidant partners, and vice versa.

This dynamic often sees a plethora of challenges including chaos, drama, tears, avoidance, and anxiety within the relationship. Triggers, unresolved trauma, abandonment issues, and codependency become entangled in a complex web of emotions, complicating the path of love.

The push and pull dynamic between an anxious attacher and an avoidant one is a common pattern observed in relationships characterised by contrasting attachment styles. Anxious attachers tend to crave closeness and intimacy in their relationships, seeking reassurance and validation from their partners to alleviate their fears of abandonment or rejection. On the other hand, avoidant attachers prioritise independence and self-reliance, often feeling uncomfortable with emotional intimacy and vulnerability. In a relationship between an anxious attacher and an avoidant one, the anxious partner may exhibit behaviours that can be perceived as 'pushing' for closeness and connection. They may seek constant reassurance from their partner, express a strong desire for emotional validation, and become anxious or distressed when their needs for closeness are not met. This can manifest in behaviours such as frequent calls or texts, seeking constant attention, or becoming overly sensitive to perceived signs of rejection or abandonment.

Conversely, the avoidant partner may exhibit behaviours that can be interpreted as 'pulling away' or creating distance in the relationship. They may prioritise their independence and personal space, avoid emotional discussions or expressions of vulnerability, and withdraw when their partner seeks closeness or intimacy. They may have difficulty expressing their emotions or connecting on a deeper level, leading the anxious partner to feel frustrated or rejected.

This push and pull dynamic can create a cycle of conflict and tension in the relationship, as the anxious partner's efforts to seek reassurance and closeness may trigger the avoidant partner's need for space and autonomy. This can lead to misunderstandings, hurt feelings, and feelings of insecurity for both partners.

An anxious-avoidant dynamic often begins with a

magnetic allure, drawing both individuals to each other like moths to a flame. Initially, the intensity of the connection can be electrifying, fueling a passionate attraction between the two parties. However, as time progresses, cracks may start to appear in the relationship.

This unravelling typically occurs when both parties are unintentional in love, lacking awareness of their own needs and failing to recognise the habits or behaviours of their partner. In the initial stages, attention is primarily focused on the intoxicating chemistry and excitement of the relationship, rather than on deeper introspection or understanding.

What does an Anxious Attacher initially find attractive in an Avoidant Partner?

1. **Mysterious Aura:** The avoidant partner's aloof and independent nature may initially seem intriguing to the anxious attacher, creating an aura of mystery.
2. **Confidence:** The avoidant partner's self-assured demeanor may exude confidence, which can be appealing to someone who seeks validation and security.
3. **Independence:** Anxious attachers may be drawn to the avoidant partner's apparent self-sufficiency and ability to thrive without constant reassurance or emotional support.
4. **Challenge:** Anxious attachers may perceive the avoidant partner as a challenge to win over, believing that they can break through their emotional barriers and earn their love and affection.

5. **Familiarity:** The avoidant partner's behaviour may resonate with patterns established in the anxious attacher's past relationships or family dynamics, feeling familiar and comfortable, albeit unconsciously.

What does an Avoidant Attacher initially find attractive in an Anxious Partner?

1. **Warmth and Affection:** The anxious partner's affectionate and expressive nature may initially provide a sense of warmth and emotional connection that the avoidant partner finds comforting.
2. **Complimentary Dynamics:**. The avoidant partner, who tends to keep emotional distance, is often attracted to a partner who is very supportive and seeks closeness (the anxious partner). This happens because the supportive behaviour of the anxious partner fills a gap for the avoidant partner, who might struggle with providing that same level of emotional engagement on their own.
3. **Reassurance Seeking:** Anxious partners often seek reassurance and validation from their partners, which may initially fulfill the avoidant partner's desire to feel needed and valued in the relationship.
4. **Emotional Intensity:** The anxious partner's intense emotional responses and expressions of love and devotion may initially be perceived as flattering and validating by the avoidant partner, boosting their self-esteem.
5. **Familiarity:** The anxious partner's behaviour may resonate with patterns established in the

avoidant partner's past relationships or family dynamics, feeling familiar and comfortable, albeit unconsciously.

In a while though, as the relationship progresses, unresolved issues and conflicting attachment styles may surface, leading to challenges and friction between the anxious and avoidant partners. Patterns of behaviour rooted in attachment insecurity become more pronounced, causing misunderstandings, emotional turmoil, and a growing sense of dissatisfaction.

Soon, conversations go from 'I find you so mysterious' to 'You're always so distant and emotionally unavailable', or 'I never know where I stand with you. It feels like you're constantly pulling away', or 'I feel like I'm always the only one putting in effort to keep this relationship going.'

The other party, the avoidants, go from 'I love that you are so loving and expressive' to 'You're always so needy and clingy. I need space to breathe', or 'Why can't you just trust me? Your constant need for reassurance is suffocating' or, 'I feel like you're trying to control me or invade my personal space', or 'You blow things out of proportion and make a big deal out of nothing.'

Why though?

It is too complex to have just one answer.

This situation often arises due to a combination of factors deeply ingrained within an individual's nature and shaped by their life experiences. Whether influenced by family background, innate disposition, social circumstances, or past relationships, these elements contribute to the formation of fears and beliefs about how relationships should or could be. This applies to both avoidant and anxious attachment styles.

1. **Family Background:** The dynamics within one's family during childhood play a significant role in shaping attachment patterns. An individual may have grown up in an environment where emotional expression was discouraged or where there was inconsistency in caregiving, leading to the development of avoidant or anxious attachment tendencies.
2. **Innate Disposition:** Some individuals may have a natural inclination towards independence and self-reliance, predisposing them towards avoidant attachment behaviours. Others may possess a heightened sensitivity to emotional cues and a strong desire for closeness and connection, characteristic of anxious attachment tendencies.
3. **Social Circumstances:** Societal norms and cultural expectations regarding relationships can also influence attachment styles. Cultural contexts that emphasise self-sufficiency and emotional stoicism may foster avoidant tendencies, while those that prioritise dependence as part of a romantic relationship, along with passionate emotional expression may encourage anxious attachment patterns.
4. **Past Relationships:** Previous experiences in romantic relationships can profoundly impact attachment styles. Traumatic or dysfunctional relationships may instill deep-seated fears of

abandonment or rejection, reinforcing anxious attachment behaviours. Similarly, experiences of feeling suffocated or engulfed in past relationships may lead to the development of avoidant tendencies as a protective mechanism.

Anxious attachers often tend to have emotional outbursts that they later regret, deal with anxiety, want immediate reassurance from their partner, and can be infamous for creating 'scenes' that are loud and draw attention, much to the horror of their avoidant partner. Much like Meghna at brunch. In a scenario like this, the avoidant partner on the other hand, say Karthik from the example above, wishes to be engulfed by the earth and because that is not possible, retreats, takes a step back (or multiple steps back), or gets defensive and shuts down, much to the disappointment of the anxious partner who only wanted a word or two of reassurance or validation of their actions or pain.

In a triggering situation, we tend to *react* (automatic and instinctive behaviour triggered by emotions or external stimuli) rather than *respond* (thoughtful and intentional action guided by reflection and consideration of the situation). These reactions are much more than just behaviour. They are a culmination of our fears, hopes, dreams, expectations, and narratives that don't align with the current triggering situation. If we don't learn to understand these reactions and learn to respond instead of reacting impulsively, it leads to the corrosion of any relationship.

Moreover, these reactions are mostly subconscious. Hence, after a reactive episode people might say things like 'I just lost it', 'It wasn't me', 'I wasn't in control', or 'I didn't mean to', but the damage by then is often already done.

I'd like to explain this and why this happens with what I call the 'Kid in the Supermarket Aisle' example.

Imagine a scenario where a child goes to the supermarket with their mom, and upon entering the chips aisle spots a packet of chips. The child eagerly asks their mom if they can have it. When their mom gently refuses, explaining that they already have snacks at home, the child's initial excitement turns into disappointment and frustration.

Feeling powerless and overwhelmed by their unmet desire, the child's emotions escalate rapidly. The kid begins to cry, shout, and even throws a tantrum in the supermarket aisle, desperately seeking to regain a sense of control and security in the face of perceived rejection.

Similarly, individuals with anxious attachment styles may exhibit behaviours characterised by urgency and emotional outbursts in their relationships. Just like the child in the supermarket, they may react impulsively and intensely when their emotional needs aren't met or when they perceive a threat to the relationship.

For example, when their partner is unable to respond immediately to a text message or cancels plans at the last minute, individuals with anxious attachment may experience a surge of anxiety and insecurity. Their fear of abandonment triggers a cascade of emotions, leading to frantic attempts to seek reassurance and validation from their partner.

In this way, the anxious individual's behaviours mirror those of the hurt child in the supermarket aisle. Both are driven by a primal need for security and acceptance, and both resort to desperate measures to cope with feelings of vulnerability and helplessness.

What would the avoidant do?

In a same scenario, when the child with an avoidant attachment spots a pack of chips and expresses interest in having it, their caregiver dismisses the request without much consideration, stating that they don't need it, and moves on without further acknowledgment.

The avoidant child, accustomed to downplaying their emotional needs and seeking independence, might initially brush off the rejection with a nonchalant attitude. However, deep down, they will feel a pang of hurt and disappointment, longing for the validation and connection that their caregiver's response lacks.

Rather than expressing their emotions openly like the anxious child, the avoidant child internalises the feelings of rejection and inadequacy. This child learns to suppress their vulnerability and mask their longing for closeness, adopting a façade of indifference to protect themselves from further hurt.

The avoidant child may proceed to distance themselves emotionally from the caregiver, avoiding seeking comfort or reassurance to *avoid feeling rejected again*. They may retreat into solitary activities or withdraw into their own world, creating a barrier between themselves and others as a defense mechanism against potential rejection or abandonment.

This emotional distancing and reluctance in engaging intimately with people who have an avoidant attachment style also shows up in their relationships with their romantic partners. Just like the avoidant child in the supermarket, they may struggle to express their emotional needs and maintain a sense of autonomy and self-sufficiency.

Aspect	Anxious Attachment	Avoidant Attachment
Expression of Needs	Expresses emotions openly and seeks validation and closeness from caregivers or partners.	Suppresses emotions and maintains distance to avoid vulnerability and maintain independence.
Coping Mechanisms	Reacts with emotional intensity and seeks external validation and support.	Responds with emotional detachment and self-reliance, avoiding reliance on others for support.
Approach to Rejection	Views rejection as abandonment and seeks reassurance and validation to alleviate anxiety.	Views rejection as expected and maintains a sense of self-sufficiency, avoiding reliance on others for emotional support.
Relationship Patterns	Tends to form dependent and clingy relationships, seeking constant reassurance and validation from partners.	Tends to form distant and detached relationships, avoiding emotional intimacy and vulnerability.
Long-Term Impact	May struggle with insecurity and dependency issues, leading to difficulties in maintaining healthy boundaries and autonomy.	May struggle with intimacy and trust issues, leading to difficulties in forming deep emotional connections and maintaining lasting relationships.

This is a chart to help you understand that both kids want similar things, but the reaction styles and coping mechanisms are different.

Adult relationships can truly thrive when we are able to see our partner's inner child. A concept derived from the body of Carl Jung's work, the idea of the 'inner child' suggests that within each adult lies a part of them that remains a child. This inner child holds on to the emotions, experiences, and innocence from those early years. Often, behaviours and emotional responses in adult relationships are influenced by this inner child, especially if there are unmet needs or unresolved issues from childhood.

Seeing our partner's inner child involves understanding and empathising with the underlying emotions, needs, and experiences that shape their behaviour and reactions in the present. This can lead us to understand the deep aspects of the relationship.

1. **Understanding Vulnerability:** Just like children, adults carry emotional wounds and vulnerabilities from their past experiences. By recognising and acknowledging these vulnerabilities in our partner, we can cultivate empathy and compassion, resulting in a deeper connection and sense of intimacy in the relationship.
2. **Empathetic Response:** When we see our partner's inner child, we are better equipped to *respond* to their emotions and needs with empathy and understanding. Rather than reacting defensively or dismissively to their behaviour, we can approach them with kindness and patience, validating their feelings and offering support. This also leads to better and effective communication.
3. **Healing and Growth:** Acknowledging our partner's inner child allows us to create a safe and nurturing environment where healing and growth can occur. By providing acceptance, we help our partner feel seen, heard, and valued, empowering them to explore and address their past wounds and traumas. (They must be willing to do the work though.)
4. **Building Trust and Security:** When we show empathy and compassion towards our partner's inner child, we build trust and security in the relationship. Only when we consciously create a

sense of safety and belonging, can we strengthen the foundation of our partnership and create a space where both partners feel free to be vulnerable and authentic.

Self-awareness is a must for any kind of change, healing, and growth. Partners must work on becoming more aware of their attachment style and its impact on their behaviour and interactions within the relationship. This includes recognising patterns of seeking reassurance and validation or withdrawal and avoidance which comes from understanding the underlying fears and insecurities driving these behaviours.

Other areas Anxious Attachers could work on that can immensely help them in personal growth and relational dynamics:

1. **Patience:** Anxious attachers struggle with feelings of insecurity and the need for constant reassurance from their partner. Cultivating patience allows them to manage their anxieties and trust in the stability of the relationship without relying excessively on external validation.
2. **Trust:** Building trust is essential for anxious attachers to feel secure in their relationship. This involves recognising and challenging irrational fears of abandonment or rejection, as well as developing confidence in their partner's commitment and reliability.
3. **Emotional Regulation:** Practicing techniques to manage their reactions and attune with emotions, such as mindfulness, deep breathing, or journaling,

can help prevent emotional escalation during conflicts or periods of insecurity. Healthy coping mechanisms help reduce dependency on external validation and builds greater emotional resilience.

4. **Boundaries and Self-Esteem:** Anxious partners could immensely benefit from setting and maintaining healthy boundaries to protect their emotional well-being and autonomy within the relationship. This involves cultivating self-esteem and self-worth independent of their partner's validation and learning to assert their needs and preferences assertively.
5. **Dating Someone Safe and Honest:** Choosing a partner who is trustworthy, reliable, and honest can provide a secure foundation for anxious attachers to feel valued and supported. Being with someone who respects their feelings and communicates openly helps alleviate anxieties and fosters a sense of emotional safety.
6. **Consistency:** Anxious attachers thrive in relationships characterised by consistency and predictability. Having a partner who demonstrates consistent behaviour and responsiveness helps reduce anxieties and builds a sense of security in the relationship.

These are things Avoidant Attachers can work on to better their quality of relationships:

1. **Willingness to Communicate:** Avoidant attachers often struggle with expressing their emotions and needs openly. Developing a willingness to

communicate allows them to share their thoughts and feelings with their partner, fostering greater intimacy and understanding.

2. **Dating Someone Safe and Reassuring:** Avoidant attachers benefit from being with a partner who is patient, understanding, and reassuring. Having a supportive partner who respects their need for space while also offering emotional support helps create a secure environment for the avoidant individual to open up and connect.
3. **Patience:** Avoidant attachers may need time to trust and fully engage in a relationship. Being patient with themselves and their partner allows them to navigate their attachment style and gradually build intimacy and trust over time.
4. **Openness to New Experiences:** Avoidant partners can benefit from cultivating a willingness to embrace new experiences and perspectives, which increases mental flexibility and openness to different points of view. This involves stepping out of their comfort zone, challenging rigid beliefs or assumptions, and exploring alternative ways of thinking and behaving.
5. **Reducing Defensiveness:** Avoidant partners can work on reducing defensiveness and resistance to feedback or criticism from their partner. This may involve learning to listen non-defensively, refraining from becoming overly reactive or dismissive, and being open to self-examination and personal growth.
6. **Addressing Feelings of Inadequacy:** Avoidant partners can confront feelings of inadequacy or

unworthiness that may contribute to their defensive or avoidant behaviours. This involves challenging negative self-talk, building self-esteem and self-confidence, and recognising their inherent value and worthiness of love and acceptance.

That being said, please remember that attachment exists on a spectrum.

Just because we identify with a certain attachment style doesn't mean we are doomed to live with it. We can change the way we show up in relationships with intentional effort and recognition of patterns that are sabotaging. Neither are anxious attachers good nor are avoidants bad. An anxious-avoidant couple *can* have a healthy bond with conscious effort, communication, patience, and understanding.

Here are some areas where an Anxious-Avoidant couple can bring in joint effort and work together:

1. **Effective Communication:** Both partners will have to work together to improve communication skills and create a safe and supportive environment for expressing thoughts, feelings, and concerns openly and honestly. This includes being direct and honest about needs and feelings instead of taking the passive-aggressive route, active listening (not fixating on a word and taking that out of context or thinking about what your reply should be when your partner is speaking and trying to actually listen to what they are saying), taking a pause to process all of that information and then responding with empathy, and validating each other's experiences.

2. **Conflict Resolution:** One sure-shot sign that your relationship is growing is when both of you can fight fairly *without* fearing conflicts. Conflicts are a natural part of any relationship. If you are willing to see past the discomfort of a conflict, it actually is a window to the deeper needs, wants, and emotions of our partners. And how do we reduce the discomfort so that we can go beyond the dreaded conflict situation? By learning *how* to fight. Volatile anxious-avoidant couples can learn constructive ways to manage conflicts and disagreements, such as by using 'I' statements. Example: Instead of saying, 'You never listen to me' which might make the other person defensive, using an 'I' statement can help express our feelings more constructively: 'I feel unheard when we discuss important topics and my opinions seem overlooked. It's important for me to feel like my thoughts are considered.' When we go into a series of 'You did this', 'You are that' and so on, our partners feel cornered and easily gets into defensive mode. This doesn't help in having a productive conversation. These partners can also start normalising taking breaks when emotions run high. However, you *have* to take the time to come back to the discussion later so that it doesn't become the elephant in the room. Another important way is to actively seek compromise or resolution through mutual understanding and respect.
3. **Building Trust and Security:** Together, couples must also absolutely prioritise actions and

behaviours that build trust and security in the relationship, such as consistent communication (not playing hot-and-cold, or disappearing for lengths of time without communication knowing that there is a person who might be worried or anxious about this absence), reliability, and showing up for each other when there is need. Without the security, commitment, honesty, and loyalty of both partners, no relationship can be sustained for long, at least not in a healthy manner. Then it doesn't matter what kind of attachment style we or our partner has. It boils down to the basics always.

Meghna is going on her first solo trip. She is excited and nervous. She can't believe she is finally doing this. Years and months of contemplation and anxiety has finally led to this day. Karthik has quietly motivated her to venture out and tick this off her bucket list.

'If you want it, go do it,' he keeps telling her.

As she takes a long, deep breath of the crisp mountain air, she video calls Karthik. She shows him the beautiful views and he smiles.

'I am glad you are enjoying your trip. Just wear more layers, I think it's cold, na?' Karthik suggests.

Meghna nods. 'Thank you for motivating me, Karthik. I feel empowered.'

Both smile, feeling connected despite the distance.

Chapter 9

I'll Huff and Puff and Blow Your House Down!

Rage, Repression, and Regulation in Relationships

There are two types of people when it comes to anger. Well, roughly.

TYPE A:

- I feel like I am going to burst with anger.
- I want to really smash something.
- I am just losing it now, please get out of my way.
- I feel like I am possessed, there is so much anger within.
- I am going to make them bloody pay.
- I don't care—I am angry right now. *proceeds to scream and curse*

I am sure you have witnessed some or all of the statements above at some point in your life in some capacity—either been on the receiving end of this or you have been the person screaming at the top of your lungs.

Or, if you disagree, then you might relate to these statements more:

TYPE B:

- I never lose my temper.
- I am not upset. I am just tired, I will sleep for a while.
- I don't feel angry at anybody, honestly.
- It's not worth making a fuss over.
- That's fine, whatever.
- I don't care enough, lol.
- It's fine, I'm fine. Don't worry about it.

Which one is better, do you think? Type B, obviously?

By now you might have come to realise that the more we stop looking at things as absolutely good or bad, or black or white, the better. Context, nuances, the greys, they all matter and are, in fact, more important.

Both sets of behaviours above are different reactions to the same thing—feelings of anger. What we see here is different coping mechanisms at play.

Type A are the kind of people who can't control their anger and may go on to make excuses for their behaviour. They may try to get away with harm done while they were angry by blaming it on their anger. Some causes for this might be:

1. **Lack of Emotional Regulation Skills:** Type A individuals lack the necessary skills to regulate their emotions effectively, particularly when it comes to managing anger. They may have difficulty identifying and expressing their feelings in a healthy

manner, leading to outbursts as a default response to stress or frustration.

2. **Underlying Issues:** The inability to control anger and the tendency to make excuses for harmful behaviour may stem from underlying psychological issues such as unresolved trauma, low self-esteem, or mood disorders like depression or anxiety. These issues can contribute to heightened emotional reactivity and difficulty managing intense emotions.
3. **Learned Behaviour:** For some individuals, patterns of anger and excuse-making may be learned behaviours acquired from childhood experiences or modeled by caregivers. If a person grew up in an environment where anger was normalised or where excuses were frequently used to justify harmful behaviour, they may internalise these patterns and struggle to break free from them in adulthood.
4. **Defense Mechanisms:** Making excuses for harmful behaviour can serve as a defense mechanism to protect the individual's self-image and avoid feelings of guilt or shame. By attributing their actions to external factors such as anger, they may temporarily alleviate their discomfort and avoid taking responsibility for their behaviour.
5. **Avoidance of Accountability:** Type A individuals may resort to making excuses as a way to avoid facing the consequences of their actions and the impact they have on others. By shifting the blame onto their anger or external circumstances, they may attempt to deflect accountability and minimise the severity of their behaviour.

6. **Fear of Vulnerability:** Behind the facade of anger and excuse-making, Type A individuals usually harbour underlying fears of vulnerability and inadequacy. Admitting fault or taking responsibility for their behaviour may require them to confront these fears and acknowledge their limitations, which can be uncomfortable and threatening to their sense of self.
7. **Limited Coping Strategies:** When faced with challenging situations or triggers, Type A individuals may have limited coping strategies beyond expressing anger in a volatile way. They lack alternative ways of managing stress or conflict, leading them to default to familiar patterns of behaviour even if they are harmful or ineffective.

Type B are the group of people who have a hard time identifying anger or admitting they are angry, and try hard to not show it. They beat themselves up when they feel anger creeping in, and might even take pride in not being an 'angry' person. The underlying causes might be:

1. **Emotional Suppression:** Type B individuals have learned to suppress their anger as a way to avoid conflict, maintain harmony in relationships, or conform to societal expectations of emotional restraint. Most importantly, they view anger as unacceptable or undesirable and go to lengths to bury or deny their feelings rather than acknowledge and express them.
2. **Fear of Confrontation:** The reluctance to show anger might also stem from a fear of confrontation

or negative consequences associated with expressing strong emotions. These individuals may prioritise avoiding conflict or upsetting others over asserting their own needs or boundaries, leading them to suppress their anger to maintain peace, mostly because they might not be able to actually handle it when a conflict arises and feel out of control.

3. **Internalised Beliefs:** Type B individuals may also have subconscious beliefs or may have received messaging from their upbringing or cultural environment that equates anger with weakness, instability, or failure.
4. **Perfectionistic Tendencies:** These individuals may also hold themselves to high standards of self-control and emotional regulation, and have unrealistic expectations by striving to appear composed, rational, and in control at all times. They may view the experience of anger as a failure to meet these standards and engage in self-criticism or self-blame for experiencing such emotions. They may also view their emotional restraint as a sign of maturity, self-discipline, or moral superiority.
5. **Avoidance of Vulnerability:** Acknowledging anger can make individuals feel vulnerable or exposed, as it requires them to confront uncomfortable truths about themselves or their circumstances. Type B individuals may resist acknowledging their anger as a way to protect themselves from feelings of shame, embarrassment, or rejection associated with vulnerability.
6. **Misguided Coping Strategies:** Type B individuals may adopt coping strategies that prioritise avoidance

or denial of anger as a way to cope with stress, conflict, or interpersonal challenges. They may convince themselves that ignoring or minimising their anger will make it go away or prevent it from causing harm to themselves or others.

Both Type A and Type B individuals, despite their different expressions of anger, share a common underlying theme of control. How?

For Type A individuals, the need for control manifests in overt expressions of anger, such as shouting, yelling, or aggressive behaviour. These individuals *may feel a sense of power or dominance when they assert themselves forcefully, using anger as a means to exert control over their environment or others.*

Trying to seek control through avoidance, suppression of anger, or displaying an 'I don't care' attitude interspersed with sarcasm is a go-to for Type B individuals. Rather than confronting difficult emotions or conflict directly, *they dismiss or invalidate the situation or the other person's feelings as a way to maintain a sense of control over their own emotional state.* By denying the presence of anger or minimising its significance, they attempt to distance themselves from uncomfortable emotions and maintain a facade of composure or detachment. They also struggle to express anger directly and often resort to passive-aggressive tactics as a way to release their frustration or assert dominance without appearing confrontational. They may use sarcasm, backhanded compliments, or subtle criticisms to undermine others' confidence or manipulate their emotions.

In both cases, the underlying motivation is a fear of losing control.

Where one fears being overwhelmed by their emotions or feeling powerless in the face of perceived threats and responds with outward displays of aggression to assert dominance and regain a sense of control, the other fears the vulnerability and discomfort associated with acknowledging and expressing anger, so they avoid it and maintain a sense of emotional distance and control over their inner experience.

Interesting, huh?

This brings me to highlight another aspect of anger—when the feeling of being in control takes over, consistently and frequently, it doesn't take long for the anger to turn into **abuse**.

Ways TYPE A individuals can display abusive behaviour:

1. **Rage:** Imagine an individual becomes enraged during an argument with their partner over a minor disagreement. In a fit of rage, they begin yelling, throwing objects, and making threats of physical harm. The uncontrolled outburst of anger escalates into abusive behaviour, creating an atmosphere of fear and intimidation for the partner.

   Example: During a heated argument about finances, Ravi becomes overwhelmed with anger and begins yelling at his partner, Arushi. In his rage, he throws his wallet across the room, narrowly missing Arushi's head. Arushi feels frightened and intimidated by Ravi's outburst, leading to a breakdown in communication and trust between them.

2. **Assault:** During a heated argument, one partner physically attacks the other by pushing, hitting, or restraining them. The use of physical force to assert dominance or control crosses the line into physical abuse, causing harm and injury to the victim.
   Example: After a disagreement at a social gathering, Veena becomes enraged and physically pushes her partner, Amit, in front of their friends. Amit is left with emotional trauma from the incident, embarrassed and hurt, causing him to feel unsafe and isolated in the relationship.
3. **Verbal Abuse:** During an argument, one partner launches into a rant of insults, belittling remarks, and uses demeaning language aimed intentionally at undermining the other's self-worth and confidence. Verbal abuse inflicts emotional harm through the use of derogatory language, humiliation, and degradation, eroding the victim's sense of self-esteem and autonomy.
   Example: During a conversation about finances which turns into a disagreement with differing POVs, Anna launches into a tirade of insults and belittling remarks aimed at her partner, Diljeet, calling him a loser and selfish. Diljeet is left feeling demoralised and worthless, damaging his self-esteem and confidence in the relationship.

Ways TYPE B individuals can display abusive behaviour:

1. **Overuse of Sarcasm or Passive-Aggression**: Constant passive aggression and belittling remarks

can be deeply damaging, even if it doesn't involve overt anger. It often stems from underlying issues such as insecurity, control, or a desire to exert power over others. Unlike overt aggression, passive-aggressive behaviour can be more subtle and insidious, making it challenging to identify and address.

Example: Veer and Suman are discussing their plans for the weekend. When Veer suggests that they could try the new restaurant in town, Suman sarcastically responds that it is the best suggestion he could make because that restaurant is a cheap one and his salary hasn't increased in the past couple of years. When Suman notices the hurt expression and silence, she tries to backtrack by saying it was a joke. Despite Suman's attempt to pass off her sarcastic comment as a joke, Veer feels stung by her harsh tone and critical attitude. He may become reluctant to share his ideas or suggestions in the future, fearing further ridicule or judgment from Suman.

2. **Silent Treatment:** After a disagreement, one partner refuses to communicate or interact with the other for an extended period, giving them the silent treatment as a form of punishment. Withholding communication or affection as a means of control and manipulation can be emotionally abusive, causing distress and isolation for the victim.

   Example: After an argument over household chores, Sunny gives his partner, Vishal, the silent treatment for several days, refusing to engage in conversation or acknowledge his presence. Vishal feels hurt and rejected by this, leading to feelings of loneliness and resentment in their relationship.

3. **Gaslighting:** When a partner seeks to avoid the discomfort of accountability and confrontation of emotions and is not ready to engage in difficult conversations, they might completely deny or dismiss any emotions or concerns raised by the other party. This behaviour creates an environment where the partner denies or minimises their behaviour, dismisses the victim's concerns, and manipulates their perception of reality. *Gaslighting undermines the victim's trust in their own experiences and feelings*, leaving them confused, doubting themselves, and dependent on the abuser for validation and approval.

   Example: After forgetting a promise made for a date night, Kushal denies ever agreeing to have decided on a date, insisting that Merin, his partner, is just assuming things and making a big deal out of nothing. Merin begins to doubt their own memory and perception of events and ends up feeling confused and invalidated which further erodes their trust in the relationship.

Let me say this loud and clear if it wasn't clear already—these behaviours that stem from anger can *destroy* relationships.

Why?

Because a healthy, fulfilling relationship can only grow where there is SAFETY.

Safety is a big pillar in a relationship for fostering trust, intimacy, and emotional well-being. Let's familiarise ourselves with different types of safety in a relationship:

1. **Emotional Safety:**
    - Feeling accepted and valued for who you are.
    - Being able to express emotions without fear of judgment or reprisal.
    - Having open and honest communication about feelings and needs.
    - Knowing that disagreements will be resolved respectfully and constructively.
2. **Physical Safety:**
    - Feeling physically secure and protected in the presence of your partner.
    - Trusting that your partner will not harm you physically or threaten your well-being.
    - Having boundaries respected and upheld, including personal space and autonomy.
3. **Trust:**
    - Having confidence in your partner's reliability and dependability.
    - Believing that your partner has your best interests at heart.
    - Feeling assured that your partner will remain faithful and honest in the relationship.
4. **Honesty and Transparency:**
    - Being truthful and forthcoming with each other, even when it's difficult.
    - Avoiding deception, secrets, or hidden agendas.
    - Sharing important information openly and willingly.

5. **Mutual Respect:**
    - Treating each other with kindness, dignity, and consideration.
    - Respecting each other's boundaries, opinions, and autonomy.
    - Avoiding belittling, demeaning, or disrespectful behaviour.

Safety is super important in any healthy relationship. By focusing on the different kinds of safety we build a strong foundation for a relationship where everyone feels safe and cared for. This makes it easier for us to trust and really connect with each other. When both people feel secure and valued, the relationship can grow stronger and both partners can thrive together.

When a partner is displaying dysregulated anger, it can compromise these aspects of safety in a relationship, leading to the one on the receiving end of this anger feeling like:

- **Walking on Eggshells:** The partner may feel like they're constantly tiptoeing around to avoid triggering outbursts or conflict. This creates a tense and anxiety-inducing atmosphere where communication becomes strained, and authenticity is stifled.
- **Breakdown in Communication:** Not being able to manage anger often leads to breakdowns in communication, with partners either shutting down emotionally or engaging in heated arguments that escalate tensions rather than resolving issues. This breakdown inhibits the open and honest dialogue

necessary for maintaining emotional intimacy and connection.

- **Lack of Trust:** Uncontrolled anger can erode trust between partners, as outbursts or aggressive behaviour may leave the other feeling unsafe or betrayed. Trust is further undermined when promises are broken, boundaries are disregarded, or honesty is compromised in the heat of anger.
- **Dishonesty and Secrecy:** In an attempt to avoid conflict or appease an angry partner, the other one may resort to conceal their true feelings or withhold information, leading to a lack of transparency and authenticity in the relationship. Over time, this can breed resentment and undermine the foundation of trust.
- **Emotional and Physical Harm:** Dysregulated anger can escalate to verbal or physical abuse, causing emotional trauma and physical harm to both partners. This damages the safety and well-being of the individuals involved, and also fuels cycles of violence and dysfunction within the relationship.

So, what can we do?

Do we feel angry or not? What can be done about anger?

I want to introduce you to the third type of people—yep, there is a TYPE C.

Type C people let themselves be angry—they acknowledge anger, the emotions that come with it and let themselves feel the heavy discomfort of anger. But they also express their anger by communicating. They know that it is possible to have a conversation AND be angry, to set boundaries WHILE being angry, and to talk WITHOUT violence or abusing while being angry.

This might sound like:

- I feel really upset about what happened, and I need to talk about it.
- I'm angry right now, but I want to find a solution that works for both of us.
- I need to set a boundary here because I'm feeling really disrespected.
- I understand where you're coming from, but I need you to listen to how I'm feeling.
- I won't tolerate being treated this way, and I need to address it.
- I need some time to cool off before we continue this conversation.
- I need you to understand how your actions are affecting me.
- I value our relationship, but I can't ignore how I'm feeling right now.

Type C people show us that it is possible to demonstrate a healthy approach to managing anger by acknowledging and accepting their emotions while also expressing them constructively. This can be done by:

1. **Acknowledging Anger:** Type C individuals understand that anger is a normal human emotion and allow themselves to experience it without judgment or suppression. Instead of denying or repressing their anger, they acknowledge its

presence and understand that it's a signal indicating something important needs attention.

2. **Feeling the Discomfort:** Rather than avoiding or numbing the discomfort of anger, Type C individuals allow themselves to fully experience the intense emotions that accompany it. They recognise that anger can be uncomfortable and even painful, but they don't shy away from it. By allowing themselves to feel the full weight of their anger, they can better understand its underlying causes and triggers.
3. **Expressing Anger through Communication:** Type C individuals understand the importance of expressing their anger healthily and constructively. Instead of resorting to aggressive or violent behaviour, they choose to communicate their feelings assertively and effectively. This involves expressing their needs, concerns, and boundaries in a clear and respectful manner, even when feeling angry.
4. **Having Conversations while Angry:** Type C individuals recognise that it's possible to engage in conversations and discussions even when experiencing anger. They understand that anger doesn't have to derail communication and that it's possible to address issues and conflicts while still feeling angry. By staying engaged in dialogue, they create opportunities for resolution and understanding.
5. **Setting Boundaries While Angry:** Type C individuals are able to assert their boundaries and

assert themselves even when feeling angry. They understand that setting boundaries is essential for maintaining healthy relationships and self-respect. Rather than lashing out or withdrawing, they communicate their boundaries clearly and firmly, even when experiencing intense emotions.

6. **Avoiding Violence or Abuse:** Type C individuals reject the notion that anger justifies violence or abusive behaviour. They understand that resorting to violence or verbal abuse only escalates conflicts and damages relationships. Instead, they seek non-violent and respectful ways to express their anger and address conflicts, prioritising healthy communication and mutual respect.

You see, anger is just an emotion with a bad reputation. This is mostly because there are more negative portrayals of anger in society and pop-culture than there are positive ones. But you know what? Anger is a NECESSARY emotion. And a NATURAL, primitive fight-or-flight response.

I want to introduce you to the concept of Positive Aggression (Ellis A. 1976. 'Healthy and Unhealthy Aggression'. *Humanitas.* 12. pp. 239–254) that was spoken of by Albert Ellis, father of Rational Emotive Behaviour Therapy (REBT), a pioneering form of cognitive-behavioral therapy.

In the context of REBT, positive aggression refers to the assertive expression of one's needs, desires, and boundaries in a manner that is respectful, constructive, and goal-oriented. Ellis believed that individuals could harness the energy of anger and aggression in productive ways to assert themselves, advocate for their rights, and pursue their goals effectively.

1. **Assertiveness:** Ellis emphasised the importance of assertive communication as a means of expressing oneself honestly and directly while respecting the rights and boundaries of others. Positive aggression involves standing up for oneself, expressing opinions and preferences, and setting clear boundaries without resorting to passive or aggressive behaviour.
2. **Rational Response to Provocation:** Rather than reacting impulsively or aggressively to perceived provocations, Ellis advocated for a rational and measured response. Positive aggression involves challenging irrational beliefs, reframing situations in a more constructive light, and responding assertively rather than reactively.
3. **Self-Advocacy:** Ellis encouraged individuals to advocate for their own needs, interests, and well-being in interpersonal relationships, professional settings, and other areas of life. Positive aggression entails speaking up for oneself, asserting one's rights and boundaries, and taking proactive steps to address issues or conflicts assertively.
4. **Problem-Solving and Conflict Resolution:** Ellis emphasised the importance of using positive aggression as a tool for problem-solving and conflict resolution. Rather than avoiding or escalating conflicts, individuals are encouraged to approach issues directly, engage in open communication,

and seek mutually beneficial solutions through assertive negotiation and compromise.

5. **Empowerment and Personal Growth:** By embracing positive aggression, individuals can experience a sense of empowerment, self-efficacy, and personal growth. Actively asserting oneself and pursuing one's goals with determination and resilience can lead to increased self-confidence, self-respect, and emotional well-being.

It's essential to recognise that anger itself is neither inherently good nor bad. Instead, it is a powerful and necessary emotion that alerts us to perceived threats, injustices, or violations of our boundaries. When appropriately channeled and managed, anger can motivate positive action, facilitate assertiveness, and promote self-advocacy.

Now, if you are a Type C, well congratulations. But if you are not, then we have some work to do.

Type A, listen up. We need to regulate and respond effectively so as to not destroy our relationships and our mental peace and take things from bad to worse. Here are some tips to help you do that:

1. **Change Your Self-Talk**: If you are an angry person, you already know it, and most probably your self-talk now sounds like 'Why can't I be less angry?', or 'Why am I like this?' Shaming yourself out of anger is only going to create more frustration. Instead, focus on the triggering event and check if it is in your direct control. There are many life-events that we think we can control but are actually beyond our individual control.

2. **That Brings Me to, Pause:** You might be wired to instinctively jump into the problem space. Resist this. Easier said than done, but even a deep breath and a minute of pausing will help you respond better. If somebody at work or your partner is just waiting for your response, tell them out loud you are taking a minute. Deep breaths and taking time out will help you assess your available options and break the familiarity of the outburst that you are used to.
3. **Get Used to Talking Like This When You Are Angry:** I mentioned changing self-talk, but how you communicate with others is as important as how you talk to yourself.

For others:

- *I need space and time to cool down when I'm feeling angry. Please respect my need for alone time.*
- *I prefer not to be approached or engaged in conversation when I'm visibly upset.*

Please give me space to process my emotions. For yourself:

- *I am committed to resolving conflicts peacefully and constructively, without resorting to verbal or physical aggression.*
- *I will seek compromise and understanding in disagreements, rather than escalating conflicts or trying to 'win' arguments.*
- *I will practice self-awareness and mindfulness to recognise early signs of anger and implement coping strategies to manage it.*

- *I will engage in activities that promote relaxation and stress reduction, such as deep breathing, meditation, or physical exercise, to prevent anger from escalating.*

Type B folks, these tips could help you accept your anger and be more direct in your communication:

1. **Increase Self-Awareness**: Begin by tuning into your body and noticing the physical sensations that accompany anger. This could include tension in the jaw, fists clenching, or a racing heartbeat. By becoming more aware of these bodily cues, you can recognise anger as it arises and address it without unconsciously resorting to avoidance or sarcasm. Begin by practising mindfulness techniques such as deep breathing or body scans to tune into your physical sensations. When you notice signs of anger arising, take a pause and label the emotion without judgment. For example, you might say to yourself, 'I'm feeling angry right now, and that's okay.' Journaling can also help explore the triggers and patterns of your anger.
2. **Acceptance of Emotion**: Consciously practice accepting anger as a natural and valid emotion, neither good nor bad, but simply a part of the human experience. This approach aligns with Acceptance and Commitment Therapy (ACT), which encourages individuals to acknowledge their emotions without judgment. For example, you can visualise anger as a passing cloud in the sky—neither good nor bad, but simply present

in the moment. Challenge the belief that anger is inherently negative or harmful. Instead, view it as a signal that something is important to you or in need of attention. Practice self-compassion by offering yourself kindness and understanding when you experience anger, rather than criticising yourself for feeling that way.

3. **Assertive Communication**: Cultivate assertiveness in expressing your feelings and needs to others. This doesn't mean lashing out in anger nor resorting to passive-aggressiveness, but rather calmly and directly communicating your concerns or boundaries. By expressing yourself openly and honestly, you can address issues before they escalate and build healthier relationships based on mutual respect and understanding. Develop assertiveness skills by setting aside time to practice assertive communication techniques, such as using 'I' statements (start your sentences when you want to address an issue with 'I feel angry because I thought we would go out and that didn't happen' vs 'You are such an irresponsible person you never keep your word.' This approach helps the other person understand your narrative better, they don't get defensive *and* it forces you to talk about your root emotions as well instead of just pointing fingers because that's easier) and expressing your needs clearly and respectfully. Start with smaller, less emotionally charged situations and gradually work your way up to more challenging ones.

4. **Lastly, Change Your Inner Dialogue to:**

- Anger is a natural emotion, and it's okay for me to feel it.
- I accept my anger without judgment or shame.
- I am capable of expressing my feelings assertively and constructively.
- I choose to respond to anger with compassion and understanding, both towards myself and others.
- I release the need to label anger as 'bad' and instead view it as a valuable source of information and insight.

Relationships are only strengthened by the good stuff (positive interactions, supportive words, loving gestures, laughter, and care), and these good things are what makes the relationship resilient enough to handle bad times. When couples consciously and consistently engage in positive interactions, they create a reservoir of goodwill and trust that can buffer against the inevitable challenges and conflicts that arise.

Dr John Gottman introduced an interesting concept called the **Emotional Bank Account in Relationships** (Gottman JM (1993). 'A Theory of Marital Dissolution and Stability'. *Journal of Family Psychology*). This concept emphasises the importance of making regular deposits into the emotional bank account of the relationship through positive interactions and gestures of love and appreciation.

Just like in the regular world, if we only keep withdrawing money from our account without depositing any, we are likely to end up bankrupt and definitely with a negative balance. The emotional bank account operates in a similar manner, except here, we are dealing with positive and negative interactions.

Let's consider fights, disagreements, or conflicts (**Negative Interactions) as Withdrawals** and words of love and support, active listening, and empathising with our partner's POV even though we don't fully understand them or agree (**Positive Interactions) as Deposits.**

Dr Gottman suggests that in order to have a fulfilling and balanced relationship, effort should be made so that for every withdrawal that occurs, there should ideally be at least five deposits to maintain a healthy balance.

These deposits can take various forms, such as expressing gratitude, showing affection, actively listening to your partner, and engaging in shared activities that bring joy and connection.

This is a good time to think whether your Relationship Emotional Bank account is abundant or just barely making ends meet.

How we respond to situations and our partners is extremely important. When we react impulsively or let our emotions dictate our behaviour, we risk damaging the trust and intimacy within the relationship. Dysregulated emotions, such as anger, resentment, or defensiveness, can erode the foundation of a relationship. Our romantic relationships bear a lot of the brunt of our dysregulated emotions and it's time we are more aware of what we do and how we speak.

Exercise: How Well Do You Understand Relationship Deposits and Withdrawals?

Situations	Impact - Withdrawal or Deposit?
Sending a thoughtful text during a stressful day at work.	
Forgetting your partner's birthday.	
Planning a surprise date night that aligns with your partner's interests.	
Frequently bringing up past mistakes during arguments.	
Dismissing your partner's new hobby as a waste of time.	
Actively asking about your partner's day and feelings.	
Showing affection in public in a way you know your partner appreciates.	
Expressing jealousy whenever your partner spends time with friends.	
Taking the time to learn and speak your partner's love language.	
Not acknowledging your partner's achievements publicly.	
Making a sarcastic comment about your partner's appearance.	
Reacting calmly and supportively during a disagreement.	
Volunteering together at a cause important to your partner.	
Accusing your partner of being too sensitive during a casual conversation.	
Celebrating your partner's promotion with a special dinner.	
Interrupting your partner frequently when they are speaking.	
Respecting your partner's wish for alone time without making them feel guilty.	
Comparing your partner unfavorably to others in social settings.	
Questioning the validity of your partner's feelings after a hard day.	
Helping your partner prepare for an important presentation.	

Instructions: Look at the statements in the Situations column. Each situation is either a Withdrawal or a Deposit. Considering whether they would add to or subtract from the emotional bank account in a relationship, write down your answer in the impact column. Some statements may be tricky, so think carefully about their impact.

Check your answers below:

1. Deposit
2. Withdrawal
3. Deposit
4. Withdrawal
5. Withdrawal
6. Deposit
7. Deposit
8. Withdrawal
9. Deposit
10. Withdrawal
11. Withdrawal
12. Deposit
13. Deposit
14. Withdrawal
15. Deposit
16. Withdrawal
17. Deposit
18. Withdrawal
19. Withdrawal
20. Deposit

This exercise is designed to deepen your awareness of the nuances of daily interactions and their effects on the health of a relationship. Keep making more deposits than what you withdraw. We don't want an empty account, do we?

Chapter 10

Mental Load

All the Work We Cannot See

I sat there, absolutely shaken, finally understanding what it was that had been irking me—why have I turned into a nagging old person? Okay, not old perhaps, but yeah, this version of me that I couldn't relate to anymore.

I had noticed myself doing less of the things that I used to enjoy before—singing at the top of my voice, just enjoying the space I had taken so long to create and curate, the always-clean house I now had. More importantly, now that I had a husband, a companion for life, a friend to multiply the good times with and a shoulder to share the lows with, why was I not feeling as happy or content as I should have been feeling after my marriage? Isn't that what society promised? Marriage was becoming a roller-coaster ride that I wanted to get out of as soon as possible, but apparently it didn't come with a stop button.

Don't get me wrong, it wasn't like I was *terribly* unhappy. I have a great partner—one who listens and understands, well, at least *tries* to understand my POV. Then why was I unhappy?

Did I marry the wrong person? Am I doomed now? Is this what marriage looks like? These questions with no specific answers plagued me day and night.

And of course, I am a 'relationship expert'. It's kind of funny that on one hand, I do have a lot of insights about relationships and how to make them better, but on the other hand, I am struggling as a newlywed. This entire situation was at first so contradictory that I noticed some shame and guilt peeking their heads out from a corner of my heart. I felt inadequate. And that added to the stress. It took me a while to remind myself that I am human. I too will have my problems. I too will falter. I too will be reactive at times and not be able to be as objective about my life and my relationships as I can be with my clients. This is a new journey for me. I am married for the first time. I am in this role for the first time. And I reminded myself of the words my therapist once told me: 'I will be only as kind to others as I am to myself.' So with that in mind, I started mindfully not being harsh to myself and letting myself be human.

I started observing the marriages around me. People seemed to have understood and accepted what marriage means. Or had they? Were they truly happy or were they just accepting a belief that this is how marriage is supposed to be? They seemed to either play the role of a dissatisfied wife who spent time with her girlfriends bitching about the husband, or the disengaged, maybe even MIA husband, chilling with friends on the pretext of work. This seemed normal and almost natural, the fate that awaits all married men and women of modern Indian society.

But deep inside, did any of them know about intimacy?

Not sex, but *intimacy*. The kind where you are vulnerable and can speak your heart out without any fear? Where you are attuned to your own emotions and ready to acknowledge and accept them? Being unable to answer these questions myself, I turned to a medium I thought would be helpful—complaining/venting.

I started by complaining and venting out in front of my mother. I told her about how my husband would leave the sink wet and the counter dripping after washing the dishes. She seemed to understand. She tch tch'ed at the thought, and resonated with my irritation, agreeing that it was indeed very irritating when the counter was left wet. But then she added, 'At least he is washing the dishes. You should be thankful.' Then she went to lament about how at one time she singlehandedly managed everything and dad was only supposed to do what he was meant to do—earn money and work.

That angered me more. I couldn't understand if my demand was irrational. Should I be thankful because my husband *at least* washes the dishes? This confusion came out in the form of nagging and passive aggressiveness in front of my husband. My husband couldn't understand. He *was* washing the dishes after all. What was the problem now? Yes, the counter was a little wet, but that's what the counter is made for, so who cares? At least, the dishes were washed, right?

He was right, but I wasn't at peace. There was an unexplainable resentment brewing internally. Even though he was doing his bit in his capacity to help me, I was still perpetually irritated, a version of myself that even I couldn't relate to.

No matter who I complained or tried to vent out to—be it, my friends, my sisters, my mother, or random people on the internet—everyone had the same kind of perspective for me—adjustment. This *is* how marriage is, it takes time. Cohabitating is a challenge and compromise is something that helps. Letting go was another huge theme of surviving a marriage.

But I didn't know what I could do to let go. You can only let go of a burden when you know what you are carrying. But all I knew was I felt tired. I felt burdened, like I was doing a lot.

This gave me something. So, with these handful of emotions, I went to my husband. My husband, who was already buried in work, looked up and smiled. I cleared my throat and launched into a conversation.

'You forgot to throw out the trash today.'

'What? No, I did throw it out,' he responded.

'No, you didn't throw the milk packet that was on the counter.'

'I got the garbage out. I didn't see any milk packets.'

'Yes, it's because you only do what you are *supposed* to do, and I end up doing most of the work.'

'What? Do you hear yourself? I don't understand. What else am I supposed to do?'

'I end up doing most things alone. I am tired.'

'Tired? I am helping you, I try to do things together, try and help you always. What else do you want me to do? I think you just have no work right now, and like picking fights with me for no reason. I truly don't have time for this right now.'

'What?' my voice broke, as involuntary tears flooded my eyes.

'Okay, what kind of work do you do around the house, tell me.' My husband has always operated more logically and rationally. 'No, go on, I would like to see how managing this house is unfair for you when I am also doing stuff around the house.'

I stood there, speechless. I could count the things I do, yes, but they did not make an overwhelming list—I have a cook to help me out, I have machines to do my washing and laundering, I have help to clean the house. Then why is it that I felt like I was burdened? I just looked at him, as silent tears ran down my cheeks. I was unable to fathom my aggression, irritation, and dissatisfaction.

It was not about the list of things I did around the house, nor was it the number of things my husband did around the house. But the problem was something much bigger. And this is when I came across the comic by French illustrator Emma Clit. It was about MENTAL LOAD—an invisible load that mostly women carry in the household. I couldn't believe my eyes. I finally felt understood and knew that my irritation, frustration, and agitation had a root. A root called the Mental Load.

Mental load refers to the invisible, yet substantial, cognitive and emotional burden that often falls disproportionately on one person in various aspects of life, particularly within households. Originating from feminist discourse, the concept sheds light on the often-overlooked responsibilities and decision-making efforts that contribute significantly to the smooth functioning of daily routines.

The term emerged during the feminist movement, recognising the imbalances in the distribution of responsibilities within households. It highlights how, in addition to physical tasks, a considerable mental burden is carried by one individual, typically a woman, who is orchestrating and coordinating various elements of daily life.

Household Examples of Mental Load:

- **Meal Planning:** While planning meals involves more than just cooking, the mental load extends to deciding on nutritious options, accommodating dietary preferences, creating shopping lists, and considering future meal schedules.
- **Managing Schedules:** Coordinating family schedules, from appointments to extracurricular activities, often becomes the responsibility of one person. This includes anticipating clashes, ensuring timely arrivals, and making adjustments as needed.
- **Remembering Details:** Keeping track of birthdays, anniversaries, and other significant dates, along with recalling preferences and special events, falls under mental load. This cognitive effort is vital for maintaining social connections and familial bonds.
- **Home Maintenance:** Beyond the physical tasks of cleaning and organising, mental load includes planning for home repairs, remembering maintenance schedules, and making decisions about renovations or improvements.
- **Childcare Coordination:** Planning and organising childcare, from arranging playdates to coordinating school activities, often rests on one individual. This includes anticipating needs, packing essentials, and ensuring a smooth routine for children.

- **Emotional Labour:** Mental load encompasses emotional labour, such as providing emotional support, mediating conflicts, and maintaining a positive atmosphere within the household. This emotional labour is essential for the overall well-being of family members.
- **Financial Planning:** While managing finances involves budgeting, paying bills, and making financial decisions, mental load extends to long-term planning, investments, and strategising for future goals.

I started researching about this term. On the one hand, I felt happy that I wasn't going crazy, nor was my marriage doomed. On the other hand, I was angry—why was I not familiar with this before? Why did the women around me not know and understand this? Why was I not taught this somewhere? After going through research and numbers I found that numerous studies and surveys consistently highlighted a stark reality: mental load within households is disproportionately shouldered by women. While the division of visible tasks might appear more balanced, the intricate web of planning, organising, and decision-making often falls predominantly on the shoulders of women.

- Various research done over the years globally [(Baxter, Janeen, and Mark Western. "Satisfaction with Housework: Examining the Paradox." *Sociology*, vol. 32, no. 1, 1998, pp. 101–20. Daminger, A. (2019). 'The Cognitive Dimension of Household Labor'. *American Sociological Review*, *84*(4), 609-633)] indicates that women often spend

more time on mental load tasks, such as planning, organising, and coordinating, compared to their male counterparts.
- The unequal distribution of mental load has profound effects on women's well-being, leading to increased stress, burnout, and a sense of being overwhelmed.
- The mental load also mostly, if not always, spills over into professional life, affecting women's career advancement and opportunities, as they juggle the demands of both work and home.

EXERCISE 1: GAUGING MENTAL LOAD

Here are some self-assessment questions to help you gauge whether you might be experiencing an unequal mental load:

- Are household and work tasks evenly distributed among all involved parties?
- Do you often find yourself taking on additional responsibilities without discussion or agreement? Is decision-making shared or concentrated in one individual or a specific group?
- Do you feel comfortable expressing your opinions and preferences in decision-making processes?
- How often are you responsible for managing the emotional well-being and needs of others? Is there an equitable sharing of emotional labour within your relationships or workplace? Are you open about expressing your feelings and needs regarding task distribution?

- Do you feel heard and respected when discussing responsibilities with your partner, family, or colleagues?
- Are you able to set and maintain boundaries regarding your time and energy?
- Do you feel guilty or anxious when delegating tasks or saying no?
- Have you been experiencing signs of burnout, such as chronic fatigue, irritability, or a sense of overwhelm?
- Are these feelings linked to specific responsibilities or areas of your life?
- How satisfied are you with your overall well-being in relation to your responsibilities? Are there specific tasks or roles that consistently contribute to feelings of dissatisfaction?

'*I help you around the house,*' is progress for modern Indian men, a statement a lot of the previous generation's men never could think of saying or even felt was necessary. But while it is progress, to all women who still feel dissatisfied after this apparent 'help', it is because the one who takes up most of the mental load is the one who still has to strategise what kind of help the partner is capable of, plan, and delegate that help too.

While the intention to 'help' with tasks is appreciated, the nuance lies in understanding the difference between *assistance* and *equitable participation*. Here is why HELP is not enough. EQUAL PARTICIPATION is:

Proactive vs Reactive Help: Merely helping when asked or intervening sporadically does not alleviate the mental load. True equity involves proactive engagement, where individuals take the initiative to identify and complete tasks without constant prompting. **Here is a comparison of *Proactive vs Reactive* help in everyday household situations—**

While meal planning:

Proactive Help: Proactively taking on the responsibility of meal planning by researching recipes, creating a weekly menu, and compiling a shopping list. This involves considering dietary preferences, nutritional needs, and upcoming events.

Reactive Help: Offering assistance with meal preparation only when prompted by the partner. While the help is appreciated, it lacks the proactivity of taking charge of the entire meal planning process, leaving the burden of planning on one person.

While taking charge of home maintenance:

Proactive Help: Recognising the need for home maintenance, the partner initiates a discussion about tasks that require attention. They schedule and oversee repairs, addressing issues before they escalate and ensuring the home is well-maintained.

Reactive Help: Only addressing home maintenance issues when they become urgent or problematic. While the assistance is valuable, a more proactive approach involves anticipating maintenance needs and planning preventive measures.

- **End-to-End Completion:** Equitable participation means taking on the entirety of a task—from planning and decision-making to execution and completion. This approach lightens the cognitive burden and ensures a more equitable sharing of responsibilities.

- **Anticipation and Initiative:** Rather than waiting for instructions, equitable participation entails anticipating needs and taking initiative. It involves actively engaging in the mental aspects of a task, not just the physical execution.
- **Shared Decision-Making:** Equitable participation extends to shared decision-making. It involves jointly contributing to discussions about family matters, plans, and daily routines, ensuring a collaborative approach to the mental load.

As I delved further into this, I wondered how I would react to letting my husband take charge of the house. Wasn't I the one who left my show and jumped from the couch when he was in the kitchen trying to slice an apple? Wasn't I the one who got anxious when I asked him to switch off the pressure cooker after three whistles and had to monitor the process even though I was part of an important meeting at that moment? Wasn't I the one who took over even simple tasks because I wanted it my way? Was I unable to ask for help? Did a part of me feel guilty for asking him to do things? Or did I have a belief that I could do it better? But, what was more important to me—which knife was used to peel the apple or enjoying the show while I was on my hard-earned break from work? Wasn't the root of my deep-seated resentment coming from not prioritising what I actually wanted to do and wanting to wear all hats and do it all perfectly?

More and more women regularly encounter internet messaging and societal expectations depicting the ideal woman as someone seamlessly managing her career, family, and personal life. Faced with these images of perfection, modern women often find themselves overwhelmed by the pressure to excel in every role without showing signs of struggle. This expectation significantly impacts their mental load as they navigate the demands of their jobs, take care of children, and maintain the household.

While the unequal mental load is undoubtedly influenced by societal expectations and traditional gender roles, it's important to acknowledge that women, too, play a role in perpetuating or even amplifying their cognitive burden. Several factors contribute to this dynamic, often rooted in personal experiences and societal conditioning:

- Women may find themselves navigating an unequal mental load due to a lack of role models who exemplify shared responsibilities. Growing up in environments where traditional gender roles are reinforced can make it challenging to envision an equitable distribution of tasks.
- Some women might hesitate to delegate tasks, especially those traditionally labeled as 'feminine' chores, due to a lack of exposure to effective delegation in their own upbringing. This hesitation can contribute to a reluctance to pass on responsibilities.
- Internalised perfectionism can lead to a rigid approach in completing tasks. Some women may struggle with delegating because they have a

specific way of doing things and fear that others may not meet their standards, adding to their own workload.
- Deep-rooted societal expectations around gender roles can lead to internal struggles. Some women may grapple with feelings of worth tied to fulfilling traditional roles, inadvertently shouldering additional mental load to conform to societal expectations.
- A fear of imperfection or a belief that tasks have to be completed to a certain standard can result in women taking on more than necessary. Intolerance to imperfection may lead to a reluctance in delegating, perpetuating the cycle of unequal mental load.

EXERCISE 2: ARE YOU ADDING TO YOUR OWN MENTAL LOAD?

Answer the following questions to assess if you might be contributing to your own mental load by not letting go, having rigid perspectives, and not trusting your partner to handle tasks.

Scoring System:
- **Rarely**: 1 point
- **Sometimes**: 2 points
- **Mostly**: 3 points

Questionnaire:

1. Do you find it hard to let your partner handle tasks without checking up on them?
    - Rarely
    - Sometimes
    - Mostly
2. Do you believe your way of doing things is the only correct way?
    - Rarely
    - Sometimes
    - Mostly
3. Do you feel anxious when you're not in control of a situation?
    - Rarely
    - Sometimes
    - Mostly
4. Do you often redo tasks that your partner has already completed?
    - Rarely
    - Sometimes
    - Mostly
5. Do you take on tasks because you think your partner will not do them properly?
    - Rarely
    - Sometimes
    - Mostly
6. Do you frequently remind your partner about their responsibilities?
    - Rarely
    - Sometimes
    - Mostly

7. Do you find it difficult to relax if tasks are left undone by your partner?
   - Rarely
   - Sometimes
   - Mostly
8. Do you feel the need to oversee every task in your household?
   - Rarely
   - Sometimes
   - Mostly
9. Do you think your partner needs your help to complete simple tasks?
   - Rarely
   - Sometimes
   - Mostly
10. Do you find yourself taking over tasks your partner started?
    - Rarely
    - Sometimes
    - Mostly
11. Do you often feel that if you don't do it, it won't get done right?
    - Rarely
    - Sometimes
    - Mostly
12. Do you struggle to delegate tasks to your partner?
    - Rarely
    - Sometimes
    - Mostly

Interpretation:

- **12-19 points**: You are doing a good job when it comes to delegation and trusting others with tasks. Keep it up!
- **20-29 points**: Sometimes you remember to relax and sometimes you are mistrusting. It's time to remind yourself often to take a back seat and be more trusting.
- **30-36 points**: You need to be more trusting and get out of your own way. Consider delegating more and trusting your partner with tasks. Communicating, and letting go of "my way is the only way to get things done" can help.

Regardless of your score, here are some things you can do to help better manage your invisible load at home, workplace, or anywhere else:

MINDSET SHIFTS: Mindset shifts are crucial on the path to change as they fundamentally alter our perceptions, reactions, and actions. By cultivating awareness, empathy, and openness to growth, we pave the way for healthier relationships. Embracing gratitude, positivity, and acceptance fosters an environment of harmony. The transformative power of mindset shifts lies in their ability to reshape thought patterns, leading to positive changes in behaviour and ultimately contributing to inner peace and fulfillment in relationships.

- **Shift 1—From Control to Collaboration:** Shift your focus from wanting to control every aspect of tasks to fostering collaboration with your partner or family members. Recognise that shared decision-making and cooperation can lead to a more balanced and harmonious environment, where everyone's input is valued.

- **Shift 2—Flexibility Over Rigidity:** Embrace flexibility and openness to different ways of accomplishing tasks. Acknowledge that there is more than one correct approach, allowing room for creativity and adaptability. This shift promotes a less rigid and more adaptable mindset, contributing to smoother collaboration.
- **Shift 3—Trust in Competence:** Cultivate trust in the competence of your partner. Recognise and believe in their ability to handle responsibilities effectively. This mindset shift not only eases the burden on you but also empowers your partner to take on tasks with confidence and capability.
- **Shift 4—Empowerment through Delegation:** See delegation not as a sign of weakness but as an empowering act. Understand that allowing others to take on responsibilities is a positive step towards shared contributions. This shift fosters a sense of empowerment for both you and those involved, creating a more inclusive dynamic.
- **Shift 5—Shared Decision-Making:** Move towards shared decision-making within your household. Value diverse perspectives and involve others in the decision-making process. This shift promotes a sense of equality, fostering an environment where everyone feels heard and valued in contributing to important choices.

- **Shift 6—Learning and Growth:** Embrace a growth mindset, acknowledging that learning to share responsibilities is an ongoing journey of personal and relational growth. Understand that each challenge is an opportunity for learning and development, fostering resilience and adaptability in both yourself and your relationships.

AFFIRMATIONS: The journey of adopting and internalising mindset shifts is greatly empowered by repetition and affirmations. Repetition, through consistent practice, reshapes neural pathways, embedding the desired shifts into your thought patterns. Affirmations, as positive declarations, act as catalysts, enhancing the impact of repetition. Together, they create a powerful synergy, fostering a profound transformation in your mindset.

Here is why repeating desired affirmations or positive statements can be so powerful:

- Regular exposure to new ideas rewires your brain, making adopted mindset shifts more deeply ingrained. Repeating positive statements reinforces these shifts, gradually replacing old thought patterns with more constructive ones.
- Consistent practice creates a positive feedback loop, making the shifts more natural and automatic over time. Declarations of positive beliefs contribute to building a reinforcing narrative, solidifying your commitment to the adopted mindset.
- Repeated application of mindset shifts builds confidence in your ability to approach challenges with a fresh perspective. Positive declarations foster

confidence, instilling belief in your capacity to embrace and sustain the desired mindset changes.

- Continuous practice contributes to a more positive and harmonious environment in your relationships. Positive declarations radiate positivity, influencing not just your internal mindset but also shaping the energy you bring into your interactions with others.
- Regular engagement builds resilience, making these shifts an integral part of your coping mechanism. Affirmations serve as reminders, encouraging consistent adoption of the desired mindset, even in the face of challenges.

Below are some affirmations that can help you in this journey. Feel free to pick and tweak however you want to. I have noticed writing your favourite ones on sticky notes and sticking them in places that you see can help you get comfortable with those ideas as your subconscious mind sees and registers them.

- I trust in my partner's abilities, and we make a great team in managing our household responsibilities.
- Delegating tasks allows me to focus on what truly matters, creating a harmonious and balanced home environment.
- Flexibility is my strength; I adapt to changes gracefully, fostering a more relaxed and enjoyable atmosphere.
- I empower others by allowing them to take charge, creating space for shared decision-making and mutual contribution.

- I release the need for perfection, understanding that each person's approach is valuable in our collective effort to share the mental load.
- Every day is an opportunity for growth, and I am open to learning new ways to balance responsibilities within our household.
- My worth is not tied to how much I can control, but to the love and collaboration that defines our shared journey.

As I progressed in my journey, I realised how much control and lack of trust I operated from. *I trust my partner to do things on their own, I trust in their capacities, and I am open to their feedback; it doesn't make me lesser*, is an affirmation that has helped me a lot.

As I now relax on the sofa, I hear my husband going about frying an egg in the kitchen. I relax, I don't have to act upon the urge of wanting to see which pan and spatula he is using. Is he using a steel spoon with the new non-stick? A voice whispers into my ear. I focus on the screen, reminding myself that I can always have this conversation if needed. Just not now. I prioritise my things at the moment. As I take a deep breath, I hear something crash in the kitchen.

I have to get up now, don't I? As I struggle to find my slippers, my husband calls out to me, 'I have it under control, it was just the salt-shaker!'

I sit back, making a mental note to talk about it later.

Additional Resources

Emotion Wheel

The emotion wheel serves as a versatile tool for enhancing emotional literacy and promoting self-awareness. One of the primary benefits of using the emotion wheel is its capacity to broaden our awareness of the subtle nuances within our emotional landscape. Often, we may find ourselves experiencing a complex blend of emotions that defy simple categorisation. The emotion wheel empowers us to navigate this complexity by offering a spectrum of feelings, each with its own distinct flavour and texture. By pinpointing the specific emotions we are experiencing, we gain clarity and insight into our inner world, allowing us to respond with greater intentionality and authenticity.

Originally created by Dr Gloria Wilcox, the wheel categorises feelings into a pie chart-like format, dividing them into seven groups: sad, happy, surprised, bad, fearful, angry, and disgusted. This tool is helpful for pinpointing the specific emotions you are experiencing at any given moment, allowing for more effective addressing and resolution. For example, if you feel generally sad, the wheel's outer bands can help you identify the exact type of sadness, such as feeling ignored. Conversely, using the wheel might reveal that a sense of inadequacy is actually rooted in deeper feelings of rejection or fear.

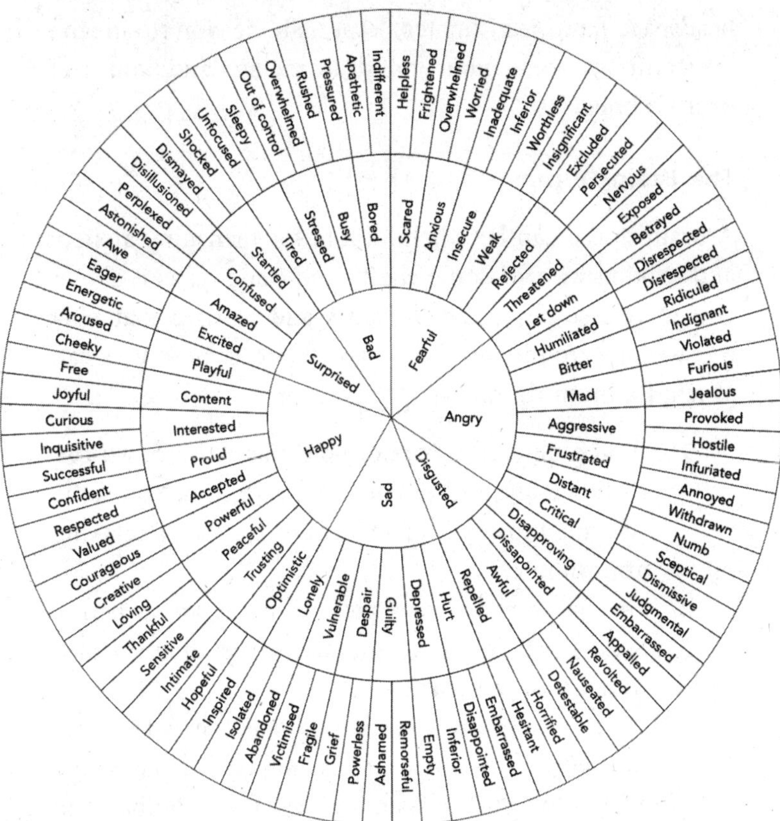

At the end of the day, take a moment to reflect. Use the wheel. What did you experience today? For instance, if you felt guilty, find 'guilty' in the middle band of the wheel. You'll find that the core feeling corresponding to guilty is 'sad', and the more specific nuanced feeling in the outer band is 'remorseful'.

Techniques for Releasing Anxiety and Controlling Overthinking

Here is a simple exercise that can really help you create headspace and feel lighter, especially if you're in the overthinking zone, your mind is racing, and you feel overwhelmed.

The Brain Dump

A brain dump can be a helpful tool for managing anxiety and making way for some clarity and stability, as it allows you to release all of the thoughts and worries that may be swirling around in your mind. Here is how you can attempt a brain dump:

1. Find a quiet and comfortable place where you can sit down and focus. You may want to put on some calming music or light a candle to create a relaxing atmosphere.
2. Grab a notebook or a piece of paper and a pen.
3. Set a timer for 10-15 minutes, depending on how much time you have.
4. Start writing down everything that comes to mind, no matter how small or insignificant it may seem. Write down all of your worries, fears, doubts, and concerns. Don't worry about spelling, grammar, or organisation—just write as fast as you can. You are writing for yourself and it need not even make sense.
5. The trick is to not rationalize—just literally let your brain take a dump. Release. Expel.
6. Once the timer goes off, stop writing and take a deep breath. You should be feeling lighter now

than when you started. You can choose to throw that paper away or burn it as a symbolic release. Please be safe if you choose to burn.

Two effective exercises to feel more grounded, connected to the present and feel in control that I swear by:

The 5-4-3-2-1 Grounding Exercise

It offers a practical and effective way to alleviate anxiety and increase mindfulness. By redirecting your attention to the present moment through sensory engagement, this exercise promotes relaxation and reduces tension in the body. Regular practice enhances self-awareness and emotional regulation, empowering you to manage stress more effectively and cultivate a sense of calm.

Tool: 5-4-3-2-1 Technique

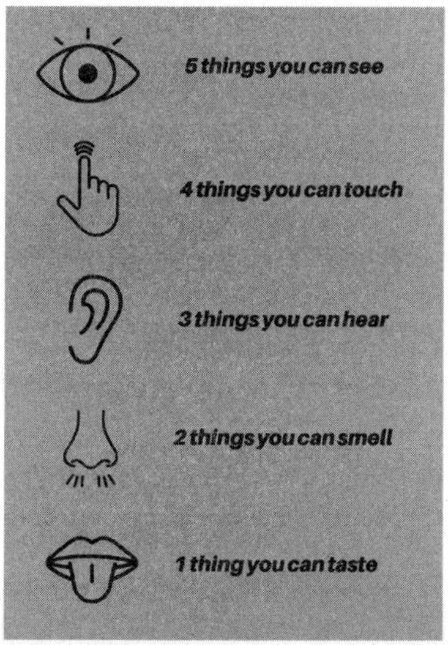

Box Breathing

Box breathing is a simple but powerful breathing technique. This serves as a tool for stress reduction and emotional balance. By regulating the breath and activating the body's relaxation response, box breathing promotes focus, concentration, and improved cognitive function. Additionally, it enhances emotional regulation and resilience, making it easier to navigate daily stressors and maintain a sense of equilibrium.

Incorporating both techniques into your daily routine can lead to significant improvements in overall well-being and mental health.

Circle of Control

It is important to understand what we can and cannot control in our lives—at work, with family and in our romantic relationships. We shed a lot of tears and spend a lot of our emotional bandwidth when we headbutt and constantly fret about things that we can't change. Instead, we should focus on things that we actually can change. This is where the circle of control comes in. Here is a diagram to help you understand.

Tool: Circle of Control

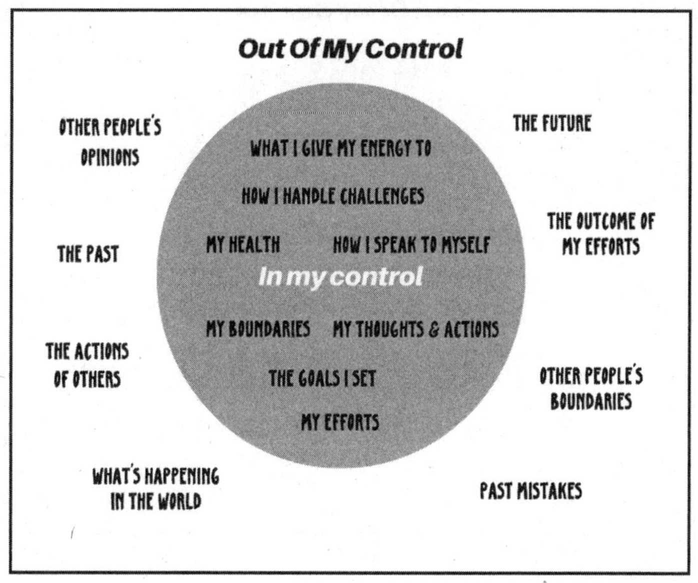

Make your OWN circle of control. There must have been times in your life when you felt stuck. Maybe you feel stuck in a situation right now. Try to identify things you can do that are in your immediate control, and identify things that are beyond your control, even if temporarily. When we identify our sphere of control in any difficult situation, we can focus our energy and attention on areas where we have agency, that leads us to a greater sense of empowerment and resilience.

Exercise : Create your own circle of control

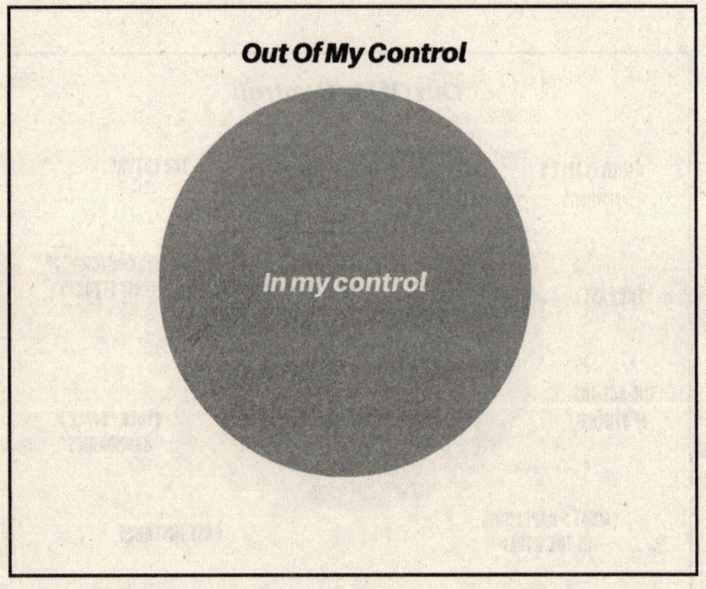

ABOUT THE AUTHOR

Kasturi Mahanta is a Counselling Psychologist specialising in Marriage and Family Therapy, a career path consciously chosen rather than being a mere coincidence. Through her platform, *@heymisstherapist*, she first started to address a gap in reliable information when in comes to building healthy relationships. This effort resulted in the creation of a conscious community with over 100K members and recognition on platforms like *Elle India* and *The Drew Barrymore Show*.